Politics and Law in Turkish Migration

TRANSNATIONAL PRESS LONDON

Turkish Migration Series

Politics and Law in Turkish Migration

Göç ve Uyum

Family and Human Capital in Turkish Migration

Conflict, Insecurity and Mobility

Politics and Law in Turkish Migration

Editors:

Ibrahim **Sirkeci**

Doğa **Elçin**

Güven **Şeker**

TRANSNATIONAL PRESS LONDON
2015

Politics and Law in Turkish Migration

Edited by Ibrahim Sirkeci, Doğa Elçin, Güven Şeker

Editorial Assistant: Therese Svensson

Printed in the United Kingdom

First edition, 2015

First Printing: 2015

Hardcover

ISBN 978-1-910781-02-9

TRANSNATIONAL PRESS LONDON
12 Ridgeway Gardens, London, N6 5XR, United Kingdom
www.tplondon.com

Contents

Acknowledgements

We would like to thank all participants of the 2014 Turkish Migration Conference held at Regent's Centre for Transnational Studies in Regent's University London who have discussed and challenged the ideas and arguments in these papers and enabled us to enhance our studies individually. Similarly, we are thankful to those colleagues who volunteered and spared time and effort to review and comment on conference abstracts and papers in this rather long journey.

As editors, we would also like to thank Regent's University London's Vice Chancellor Professor Aldwyn Cooper for his continuous support and encouragement along with many other colleagues for hosting and making Turkish Migration Conferences a pleasant and successful scholarly gathering. We also thank *Ria Financial* for their generous support to Regent's Centre for Transnational Studies and sponsoring the best paper prizes at the conference along with *Migration Letters* journal.

We would like to thank to our research assistant Therese Svensson for her meticulous work in copy-editing the manuscript and accommodating our impatience and endless requests at times. Finally we would like to thank our families and friends without whose help and continuous support this book would never have been completed.

About the authors

Necdet Coşkun Aldemir is a PhD candidate at the Institute of Sociology – Faculty of Social Sciences and Cultural Studies Justus-Liebig-University Giessen, Germany. His research interests encompass social theory, social movements, transnational migration, Sociology of everyday life, media anthropology, and digital communication technologies.

Süreyya Sönmez Efe is a PhD Researcher and an Associate Staff working with the Politics and Applied Global Ethics Group at Leeds Beckett University. Her scholarly interests include Human Rights, Social Justice, European Politics, Turkish Politics, Migration and Citizenship, Kant's ethics and cosmopolitanism. Her current research looks into the legal rights of migrant workers in Turkey and Turkish Immigration Policy. Before joining Leeds Beckett University, she worked at Amnesty International UK Section as a researcher where she actively involved in a number of campaigns and lobbying of the parliament. Currently she teaches on Politics, Ethics and Justice and on Social Research Methods modules at Leeds Beckett University.

Dr Doğa Elçin is currently Assistant Professor at Atılım University Faculty of Law Department of Private International Law, in Ankara, Turkey. Prior to this she was an attorney at law with the Ankara Bar Association. Her publications include: "The Law Applicable to Individual Employment Contracts and Collective Agreements". She completed her Ph.D. in Private International Law at Ankara University in 2011.

Dr Deniz Eroğlu is a Lecturer in Public Finance Department in Trakya University. She is also teaching Migration Policies and Actors course at Public Administration Institute for Turkey and the Middle East (TODAIE). She holds a PhD and a Master degree in Government Department, University of Essex; as well as a BA in International Relations from Hacettepe University. Her PhD thesis is 'The Making of Asylum Policies in Turkey: Analysis of Non-Governmental Organizations, Political Elites and Bureaucrats'. Currently her fields of academic interest include asylum policies of Turkey, mass migration movements and burden sharing initiatives.

Dr Jessica Guth is the Head of Law at the University of Bradford, UK. She joined the School of Law as a Lecturer in 2007 after working as a researcher for Leeds University for 3 years. She has an LLB (Hon) from Leicester University, completed the Legal Practice Course at Nottingham Trent University and an MA Social Research at Leeds University. Her PhD was awarded by the University of Liverpool in 2011 for the thesis titled 'Evaluating Law and Policy in the Context of Doctoral Mobility in the European Union'. Dr Guth's research interests are in the areas of European Union Law, particular EU Citizenship and Gender and the EU Institutions as well as in Legal Education.

Mine Karakuş, born in Istanbul, Turkey, holds BA in Sociology from Bogazici University and a Masters degree from European Studies Program at Sabancı University. Currently she is working as a Research Assistant for the International Center for Civil Society Studies and Practices at the Anadolu University. She is currently a PhD candidate and conducting a field research on refugees and asylum seekers who are living in the city of Eskişehir, Turkey.

Prof Philip L. Martin is Professor of Agricultural and Resource Economics and the Chair of UC Comparative Immigration & Integration Program. Philip Martin received his degree from the University of Wisconsin-Madison in 1975. His research focuses on: immigration, farm labour, and economic development. Martin is Chair of the University of California's Comparative Immigration and Integration Program, and editor of the monthly Migration News and the quarterly Rural Migration News. In the U.S., he was the only academic appointed to the Commission on Agricultural Workers to assess the effects of the Immigration Reform and Control Act of 1986. He received UC Davis' Distinguished Public Service award in 1994. He assessed the prospects for Turkish migration to European Union between 1987 and 1990, evaluated the effects of immigration on Malaysia's economy and its labour markets in 1994-95, and Martin was a member of the Binational Study of Migration between 1995 and 1997.

Annalisa Morticelli is a PhD candidate at the Faculty of Law, in Hamburg Universität, Germany. Her PhD focuses on the protection of human rights of irregular migrants in EU. Annalisa is a Civil Mediator in Italy and collaborates as research coordinator at the EST Think Tank, in Amsterdam. She was a visitor researcher at the School of Law, in Bradford University, UK. She achieved her Master's degree in Law (Hon) and a Master's of Advanced Studies at Università degli Studi of Torino, Italy. She conducted her internship in a Torino's legal firm and several stages at the Court of Torino.

Dr Devrimsel Deniz Nergiz completed her doctoral thesis at the Bielefeld Graduate School in History and Sociology, Faculty of Sociology at Bielefeld University, Germany. She is the author of *I Long for Normality, A Study on German Parlamentarians with Migration Backgrounds* (Springer, 2014). She has also co-authored several articles with Anna Amelina, Thomas Faist and Nina Glick Schiller to appear in journals including *Ethnic and Racial Studies*.

Dr Selcen Öner is Assistant Professor at Bahçeşehir University (İstanbul) at the Department of EU Relations. Her research interests are Turkey-EU relations, European identity, EU politics, civil society in Turkey, Turkish foreign policy and Europeanization. Some of her recent publications are: *Turkey and the European Union: The Question of European Identity*, (Lexington, 2011); "Internal Factors in the EU's Transformative Power over Turkey: The Role of Turkish Civil Society", *Southeast European and Black Sea Studies*, 14(1) (2014); and "Europeanisation of Civil Society in Turkey during the Accession Process to the European Union", In: Çiğdem Nas and Yonca Özer (eds.), *Turkey and the European Union: Processes of Europeanisation* (Ashgate, 2012).

Emily Joy Rothchild, PhD Candidate from the University of Pennsylvania, is completing her dissertation on the micro- and macro-political integration of migrant descendants at the Hamburg HipHop Academy. Having completed ethnographic fieldwork in Zanzibar, Dresden, Chapel Hill, Philadelphia, and Hamburg, Rothchild's research interests' center on migration, Islam, social integration, gender, Turkish-Germans, and hip-hop. Rothchild holds a Master of Arts in the Anthropology of Music from the University of Pennsylvania and is a visiting fellow at Hamburg's Research Center for Media and Communication.

Prof Ibrahim Sirkeci is Ria Financial Professor of Transnational Studies and Marketing and the Director of the Regent's Centre for Transnational Studies (RCTS) at Regent's University London (UK). He holds a PhD in Geography from the University of Sheffield (UK) and a BA in Political Science and Public Administration from Bilkent University (Turkey). Prior to joining Regent's University London, Sirkeci had worked at the University of Bristol. His main research areas are Human Mobility, Transnational Marketing and Consumers, Labour Markets, Remittances, and Segmentation. He is the editor of several journals including *Migration Letters* and *Transnational Marketing Journal*. His books include *Transnational Marketing and Transnational Consumers* (Springer, 2013), *Migration and Remittances during the Global Financial Crisis and Beyond* (World Bank, 2012 with J. Cohen and D. Ratha), and *Cultures of Migration, the global nature of contemporary mobility* (University of Texas Press, 2011 with J. Cohen) which was named 'Outstanding Academic Title' by Choice magazine in the USA. He has been chairing the *Turkish Migration Conference* series since 2012.

Dr Güven Şeker is Associate Professor of Public Administration and the Director of Celal Bayar University Population and Migration Research Centre, Manisa, Turkey. He has moved to academia after a long service at Security Department serving in Manisa, Izmir and Van provinces where he had dealt with border crossings and irregular migration. He has also served in UN mission in Sudan during his time with the Security Department. He has also carried out research in London while he was a post-doctoral visiting researcher at Regent's University Centre for Transnational Studies in 2013. His research focuses on country of origin, migration governance, and integration.

Nils Witte is PhD Fellow at Bremen International Graduate School of Social Sciences (BIGSSS). In his dissertation he examines the role of symbolic boundaries for naturalization intentions of Turkish residents in Germany. In 2014 he was DAAD funded visiting student at the European University Institute. He studied sociology and political science in Mannheim and Florence and graduated from the University of Mannheim in 2011.

Introduction

Philip L. Martin and Ibrahim Sirkeci

Traditional source countries are rapidly becoming destination countries as international human mobility diversified. There are many countries with surplus populations despite increasing efforts to regulate international migration. The number of international migrants, defined as persons living outside their country of birth at least a year, more than doubled between 1980 and 2013, from 103 million to 232 million, so that migration rose faster rise than the global population (See http://esa.un.org/migration/). The number of international migrants is projected to top 400 million by 2050. Turkey, once a major source country, has turned into an immigration destination over the last decade or so. The addition of 2 million Syrians, most of whom are likely to stay much longer than intended, has dramatically increased the size of foreign born population in Turkey. It is estimated that about 40% of world's movers live in developing countries whilst the remaining 60% live in the industrialised countries. Recently, the largest international population movements are between developing countries of the South. Turkey, as in many respects, sits in between these crossroads of South-South and South-North migration routes as a country of origin, country of destination, and as a transit country.

Migration is as old as humankind wandering in search of food, but international migration across defined and policed national borders is a relatively recent development. It was only in the early 20th century that nation-states developed passports and visas to regulate the flow of people across their borders (Torpey, 1999). Nevertheless, international migration is the exception, not the rule, and most people do not want to move away from family and friends.

Second, governments have significant capacity to regulate migration, and they do, as evidenced by long lines of people outside consulates seeking visas and large agencies that patrol borders and check on foreigners inside countries. One item considered by many governments when deciding whether to recognize a new entity that declares itself a nation state is whether it is able to regulate who crosses and remains within its borders.

One reason that international migration is likely to increase is because there are more national borders to cross: the number of nation states increased from 43 in 1900 to 193 in 2000 (Lemert, 2005: 176). Each nation-state distinguishes citizens and foreigners, has border controls to inspect those seeking entry and deter unauthorized entries, and determines what foreigners can do while inside the country, whether they are tourists, students, guest workers, or immigrants.

Nevertheless, the key drivers for international human mobility are two inequalities coupled with three revolutions. The demographic inequality: Almost all population growth occurs in the world's 170 poorer countries, while the population of the 30 richer countries is expected to remain at about 1.2 billion. The economic inequality: Worldwide GDP was $75 trillion in 2013, an average over $10,000 per person a year. The 30 high-income countries had a sixth of the world's people but two-thirds of the world's economic output, an average $40,000 per person per year, 10 times more than the $4,000 average in the poorer 170 countries (World Bank, 2014). Thus, especially young people are motivated to cross national borders to earn wages that are 10 times higher than they can earn at home. Even in the Syrian crisis where people escape violence, one can notice the fact that Turkish GDP per capita is three times higher than that of Syria, which plays a role in destination choices.

The three revolutions making international mobility more likely are improvements in communications, transportation, and rights over the past half century. The communications revolution highlights the ease with which information flows over national borders. In the mid-19th century, when literacy rates in rural areas were often low, immigrants in the US would write so-called American letters to friends and relatives describing opportunities and send the letter on a weeks- or months-long trip to Europe, where the recipient would have to find someone literate to read it and respond. Today, with mobile phones and the internet, some studies suggest that workers in Mexico may learn about job vacancies in Los Angeles workplaces sooner than Californians (Waldinger & Lichter, 2003).

The transportation revolution means lower cost and ease of travel. In the mid-18th century, many British migrants to what became the US who could not afford the one-way fare. To board ships, they signed indentured-servant contracts that obliged them to work four to six years for whoever met the ship in Philadelphia or New York and paid the captain. Today, the one-way cost of traveling legally to almost anywhere in the world is less than $3,000, and even migrants who pay smugglers $20,000 or more to get into higher wage countries can usually repay this cost in less than two years (Kwong, 1999).

The rights revolution refers to the post-WWII international human rights conventions and the expansion of political, social, and economic rights in most countries. Human rights conventions grant basic civic rights to all persons, labour conventions call for all workers to be treated equally in the workplace, and national laws often grant at least some political, social, and other rights to all residents. One consequence of this expansion of individual rights is that, once inside a country, governments may have difficulty removing foreigners who want to stay.

Hence policy makers grappling with unwanted migration face a great challenge, since they can do little in the short-term to reduce demographic and economic inequalities, and they do not want to roll back communications and transportation revolutions that facilitate cross border mobility. Then the only instrument available to alter migration flows quickly is rights. Reducing migrant rights is often the policy tool used to deal with migration crises, as when EU states adopted the Dublin convention in the early 1990s. However, Turkish government has granted more rights to new arrivals from Syria, which normally does not recognize non-Europeans as refugees due to Turkey's geographic reservation to the 1951 Geneva Convention.

More typical of government responses were policies adopted to deal the large influx of asylum seekers as a result of the break-up of the ex-Yugoslavia, the fall of Communism, the military intervention and the Kurdish unrest in Turkey[1]. Fearing a backlash against foreigners among voters, several countries tightened their otherwise liberal asylum laws during the 1990s and 2000s (Martin, 2004a and 2004b). Many European states, then settled on a compromise that

[1] For migration of Kurds from Turkey to Germany, see Sirkeci (2003).

preserved the constitutional right to asylum but made it more difficult to foreigners to apply. This is followed by stricter visa regulations, sanctions on carriers of movers, and safe countries list, and so on (Hailbronner, 2010).

Another attempt to manage migration by adjusting rights is via restricting the access of immigrants to welfare benefits. In the US and the UK, there were allegations of 'benefit tourism,' when migrants received benefits soon after their arrival. In the US, the access of immigrants to benefits was reduced (Migration News, 1996 and 1999), but the number of migrants was not reduced, an example of a trade off between migrant numbers and rights that was resolved by reducing rights (Ruhs & Martin, 2008).

The United States is a nation of immigrants. Under the motto "e pluribus unum" (from many one), US presidents frequently remind Americans that they share the experience of themselves or their forbearers beginning anew in the land of opportunity.[2] The Turkish public discourse also proudly acknowledges the Turks' wandering ancient roots. However, instead of welcoming all foreigners, there is a desire to select immigrants rather than to have Syrians select Turkey. The US had barred certain types of immigrants in the 1880s and limited entries with quotas in the 1920s (Martin, 2010). Similar qualitative and quantitative quota systems regulate immigration to the US and other countries.

Half of the unauthorized eluded apprehension at the Mexico-US border, while the others entered legally but violated the terms of their visitor visas by going to work or not departing.[3] Turkey has apprehended about a million irregular movers in the last two decades and deported most of them (Seker and Ozer, 2014; Sirkeci and Martin, 2014). Countries that provide too few opportunities for legal migration often have more irregular migrants.

---

[2] The exceptions are Native Americans, slaves, and those who became US citizens by purchase or conquest, such as French nationals who became Americans with the Louisiana Purchase, Mexicans who became Americans with the settlement ending the Mexican War, and Puerto Ricans who became US citizens after the US victory over Spain in 1898.

[3] US immigration statistics distinguish between Entries Without Inspection (EWIs) and overstayers, meaning those who entered legally and violated the terms of their entry or did not depart. About 55 percent of the 11 million unauthorized foreigners in 2012 were EWIs.

Unauthorized migration is the major policy concern in the US, and debates over how to prevent such migration and deal with unauthorized foreigners reveal a major division between Republicans and Democrats. Many Republicans, especially in the House, prefer an enforcement-first approach, meaning more agents and fences on the southern border with Mexico and a requirement that US employers submit data on newly hired workers to the government to prevent unauthorized workers from getting jobs. President Obama and many Democrats prefer "comprehensive immigration reform" that includes more border and interior enforcement to discourage the entry and employment of unauthorized foreigners, but also includes a path to legal immigrant status.

Turkey, which now has a fairly open southern border with Syria, can expect more immigration. Even if the Syrian crisis ends, many Syrians are likely to settle in Turkey, and their presence can provide a magnet for more Syrians to move to Turkey. Thus, there is still much to learn from the US experience regarding Mexican immigration and its impact on migration policy. This edited volume is a timely attempt to map political and legal geography of Turkish international migration experience.

***

This edited volume is organised in two broad sections, first of which reviews the legal frameworks and policy making, whereas the second focuses on various aspects of political participation among Turkish diaspora populations with a particular emphasis on Germany.

Morticelli and Guth appraises the European Union (EU) legal framework on irregular migration from third countries into the EU. They argue that the system is not effective and there is no systematic or coherent approach to irregular migration in the European Union. Eroğlu points that it was important to fill the legal loophole in Turkish legislation to regulate international protection and to have an international protection system that is compatible with human rights. She draws upon interviews with bureaucratic elite and different actors participated the process of creating the new Foreigners Law in Turkey. Elçin underlines that non-refoulement, one of the fundamental principles of international refugee law, has been regulated for the first time in Turkey by the Law on Foreigners and International Protection No.6458 in 2014. She compares Turkish national law to international refugee law with reference to the principle of non-refoulement. Efe debates another aspect of the law; the legal status of migrant workers in Turkish immigration policy after the 2008 global financial crisis with a particular emphasis on human rights.

Migrant experiences are discussed in significantly different areas in the second half of the book. Nergiz assesses the role of being someone with migration background in German politics and investigates whether such background has been an advantage of disadvantage for Turkish politicians drawing upon 14 qualitative interviews. Following a similar line of investigation, Vermeulen and Doğan map the personal strategies of current politicians of Turkish origin (second generation immigrants) in gaining access to the local political systems and dealing with pressures in Berlin and Amsterdam. Rothschild tracks the adverse changes in the integration process and debate in Germany in the aftermath of the 9/11. She argues macro-political integration is a two-sided process, necessitating migrants' acknowledgement of local customs and norms but also requiring acceptance and understanding from the receiving society. Witte examines immigrants' perception of symbolic boundaries reflecting on a series of in-depth interviews conducted with Turks living in Hamburg. Aldemir investigates the potential of social media to play a role in migrants' transnational political activities, specifically for the second generation's participation. Taksim Gezi Park protests are taken as an example for the second generation's participation in transnational political activities. Karakuş, again adopting qualitative approach, explores the role played by citizenship preferences in political integration of the German-Turks. In the final paper, Öner analyses the role of Turkish community organisations in Berlin, the challenges regarding their involvement and influence in German politics, their perceptions about Turkey's EU membership bid and their role in Turkey-EU relations.

Chapter 1: Irregular Immigration in the EU Legal Framework: Where are the Human Rights?

Annalisa Morticelli and Dr Jessica Guth

This paper considers the European Union (EU) legal framework which deals with irregular migration from third countries into the EU. It begins by outlining the legal frameworks focusing on three areas, which arguably impact most directly on irregular migrants: Border Controls, Human Trafficking and Illegal Employment. The paper aims to highlight some of the issues arising from the legal framework. In particular it questions the continued focus on provisions which stigmatise migrants as criminals and thus continue to foster distrust between Member States and migrants. It examines the provisions in Directive 2011/36/EU and considers the extent to which they have addressed some of the concerns raised in relation to previous legislation in this area. This paper argues for a more principled approach which is based on a more holistic consideration of migration policies in the EU, which takes more explicit account of human rights based theories of migration increasing the use of effective legal instruments and humanitarian operations.

Irregular migration in the EU: The legal response

Over the last decade or so the EU has launched a series of legal provisions and policy documents containing the guidelines, objectives and legal instruments with which to operate in the fight against irregular immigration from third countries (see Morticelli with Guth, 2011, Iancou, 2011, Hailbronner 2000, Ross, 2013, Sawyer, 2011, Stoivocivi, 2010). The key aim seems to be to combat the aiding and abetting and exploitation of irregular immigration by criminal gangs through the trafficking of human beings and to disincentivise the use of irregular migrants as a cheap labour force (Cellamare, 2012). Some efforts have also been made to address the issues which act as '*push factors*' in the countries of origin so as to reduce irregular migration flows and to strengthen border controls and migration management processes (see Castel and Miller, 2010, Kivisto and Faist, 2010,

Koser, 2010). This paper briefly outlines the key legal provisions in these areas.

Border controls

It is of course true that the EU does not have competence to legislate on external border control. Member States remain responsible for the monitoring and surveillance of their external borders as well as for setting their own immigration policies vis-à-vis third country nationals.[1] That is not to say that the EU has no role to play or no influence in this area. EU policy in the field of external borders of the European Union is focused on supporting Member States in the management of border controls and ensuring a high and uniform level of control on persons and surveillance, as a prerequisite for creating a space of freedom, security and justice. To help achieve that aim it created the European Agency for the Management of Operational Cooperation at the External Borders of the Member States of the European Union "FRONTEX" (Regulation 2007/2004). In legal terms, the field of border control is governed by the Schengen Borders Code (Regulation 562/2006), which defines rules for crossing the external borders and internal border controls. It applies to any person crossing any borders of a Member State. External border controls for EU citizens or other persons enjoying the right of free movement within the EU are very simple and fast, relying on straightforward checks of personal identification cards. Non-EU citizens are subject to thorough checks relating to verifying identity, conditions of entry and where necessary residence permits and other relevant documentation[2]. In 2009 the EU created the Visa Code (Regulation 810/2009), which regulates the conditions and procedures for issuing visas for short stays and transit through Member States and

[1] There are of course some notable exceptions in relation to specific groups of 3rd country nationals such as for example those falling within the scope of Council Directive 2005/71/EC of 12 October 2005 on a specific procedure for admitting third-country nationals for the purposes of scientific research OJ L *289 , 03/11/2005 P. 0015 – 0022.*

[2] In May 2011 the European Commission, in light of recent events in North Africa which increased the influx of immigrants into the EU, proposed some amendments which provide for the introduction of a safeguard clause that would allow, under certain exceptional conditions, the temporary reintroduction of visa requirements for nationals of a third country who do not normally require one.

associated States by applying the Schengen *acquis*. It requires nationals of third countries to be in possession of visas when crossing the external borders of the EU and for some countries to be in possession of an airport transit visa for passage through the international transit areas of airports of Member States.

Moreover, the European Parliament recently adopted the Regulation establishing rules of surveillance in FRONTEX coordinated joint operations. The content of this Regulation will be addressed subsequently with more details.

A further development to consider is the European Border Surveillance System "EUROSUR" established in 2011 and becoming operational on 2 December 2013. It aims to reduce the number of irregular migrants entering the EU undetected, help member states to react faster to incidents regarding undocumented migrants and cross-border crime. Its main pillars are the '*national coordination centres'*, in which all authorities responsible for border surveillance are required to coordinate their activities. It will be operational in a total of 30 countries. However, critics have described this measure as extremely expensive with costs around 144 billion euro, discriminatory and anti-immigrant and that it will only be justified if there is a substantial decrease in the number of deaths involving migrants attempting to get into the EU.

Moreover, it is interesting to underline that given the Greek EU presidency in the first half of 2014, the Greek Prime Minister Antonis Samaras started discussions with his counterparts in Italy and Malta on a common approach towards irregular migration (PICUM 2013). The three prime ministers called for a more concrete European strategy in order to address irregular migration. Antonis Samaras underlined that the strengthening of FRONTEX and repatriation of undocumented migrants are the key points at this stage.

Human Trafficking

Another important area to consider in relation to irregular immigration is the EU's fight against human trafficking (Triandafyllidou and Maraoukis, 2012). The Council action plan on trafficking in human beings (European Council, 2002) and the Commission Policy Plan on legal immigration (European

Commission, 2005) are examples of developing coordination and cooperation mechanisms and developing guidelines for data collection in order to better understand this area. Through its development policy the Commission stated that they have to continue funding measures addressing the factors that make some people vulnerable to trafficking, such as poverty, discrimination and lack of access to basic and higher education.

Directive 2004/81/EC supplements a range of European level measures designed to combat trafficking in human beings, including Council Framework Decision 2002/629/JHA (now replaced by Directive 2011/36)[3] on combating trafficking in human beings and Council Directive 2002/90/EC defining of unauthorized entry, transit and residence. The Directive defines the conditions for granting residence permits of limited duration to non-European Union nationals who are victims of human trafficking or the subject of an action relating to the smuggling of people and who cooperate in the fight against these crimes. The permit may be granted to non-EU nationals even if they have irregularly entered the territory of an EU country. EU countries may make the issuing of the permit conditional upon participation in these programs. The residence permit may be withdrawn for reasons relating to public policy and national security, abuse and fraud. It may also be withdrawn if the victim renews contacts with those suspected of committing the offences or ceases to cooperate or when the proceedings are discontinued. A communication of 2010 complains of some deficiencies in the correct application of the Directive: The number of victims of trafficking in human beings is much higher than the number of temporary residence permits issued on the basis of this Directive per year. Consequently, the impact of the Directive in protecting victims and dismantling traffickers' networks seems to be limited. EU countries should provide victims with better access to information on the opportunities provided by the Directive. Furthermore, they should fully comply

[3] 2002/629/JHA, Council framework Decision of 19 July 2002 on combating trafficking in human beings, *O.J.L. 203*, 1 August 2002, p.1-4. Although the Framework Decision has now been replaced by Directive 2011/36, it is worth discussing it here as the Directive only recently passed its implementation date and has not yet been fully evaluated. We turn to a more detailed consideration of the Directive below.

with the provisions concerning treatment of victims during the reflection period. The carrier's liability Directive 2001/51/EC and Council Directive 2004/82/EC on the obligation of carriers to communicate passenger data are also relevant instruments in the fight against human trafficking as they put some onus on carriers to ensure they are not making it easy for traffickers and are collecting relevant data which may be helpful in tackling the issues raised.

The law relating to trafficking is based around criminalization of trafficking but does not take enough care to ensure that it does not criminalize those being trafficked. For example, the legal provisions presume that victims of trafficking are in a position to report their traffickers and then act as a witness in any prosecutions. This is likely to grossly underestimate the power traffickers have over their victims and their families. The fact that residence permits can be granted to victims of trafficking by regularizing their status in the host state is to be welcomed. However this provision is significantly watered down by the fact that these permits can be withdrawn where a victim renews contact with the traffickers or does not cooperate in investigations and prosecution. This places a significant burden on the victims of trafficking and does not demonstrate an adequate understanding of their position and the phenomenon of trafficking of human beings. In other words, the current approach pays insufficient attention to the victims' human rights and need for support and instead puts them at risk of being re-branded as criminals and illegal even after they have managed to achieve regular status.

It is necessary to highlight that some improvements on this issue have been introduced by the Directive 2011/36/EC, which focus more on human rights than previous legislation in this area. This Directive will be considered in more detail below.

Illegal Employment

The final set of legal measures we want to consider here relates to illegal employment. According to research, illegal employment often follows trafficking because the same smugglers offer illegal work to being trafficked; thus combating such employment will help to combat trafficking (Berecht and Tuncay, 2013). In this regard, Directive 2009/52 was enacted which requires Member States to prohibit the employment of illegally staying non-EU nationals. Member States must ensure that infringements are subject to effective, proportionate and dissuasive sanctions. The Directive provides for minimum common standards on sanctions and, in serious cases, criminal penalties against employers of irregular migrants. The Directive also sets out minimum administrative requirements that employers have to adhere to when employing TCNs. This Directive also provides for the facilitation of complaints and the specific provision regarding the obligation to inform the victims and provide them the necessary assistance to achieve the effective recovery of outstanding wages and contributions. The financial sanctions may be reduced for individuals employing illegally staying non-EU nationals for private purposes, provided that the working conditions were not exploitative[4].

The rationale of combating illegal employment of irregular immigrant workers and trying to develop a parallel market for regular workers (Staples, 1999), starts from the consideration that the action against irregular immigration and illegal residence should include measures to fight the pull factor of opportunity. Facilitating the regularization of those who enter a Member State for work purposes and at the same time punishing the employers who take on illegal immigrants in the EU, is considered an effective strategy for the development of legal and the prevention of irregular immigration (Block and Chimenti, 2011). However, the provisions do tend to stigmatize migrants as criminals: they ignore the fact that many have no choice but to work illegally and may not have the skills, knowledge or human capital to seek help or change their situation. We will return to these issues below.

---

[4] Member States must put in place the necessary mechanisms where by illegally employed non-EU national may claim any outstanding remuneration from their employers. The non-EU nationals must be informed of their rights before their return is enforced. Member States must ensure that employers are also, if appropriate, subject to other measures. Moreover, in the cases indicated in the document, an intentional infringement constitutes a criminal offence. Those working in particularly exploitative conditions may be issued residence permits for the duration of their proceedings on a case-by-case basis, under arrangements comparable to those provided for by directive 2004/81/EC on the residence permit issued to third-country nationals who are victims of trafficking in human beings and who cooperate with the competent authorities.

Problems with current legal framework

The EU legal framework has been criticised on many levels and we do not intend to set out those debates here. However, we examine two key problems which are in need of further consideration and these two problems, in our view, lead to a third and fundamental flaw in the legal framework in this area (see also Estrada-Tank, 2013). The first issue is that there is no coherence in EU migration policy generally and that even when considering only those law and policy provisions relating to irregular migration directly, there cannot be said to be clear strategic aims and objectives which are mutually supportive. As Pop put it: '*At present, the EU immigration policies are marked by ambivalences and ambiguities. These ambiguities are rooted in contradictory policy logics, especially those of criminal justice, labour market, foreign policy and development, and gender equality policies.*'(Pop, 2008). This lack of coherence is explored further below.

The second problem arising from the legal framework on irregular migration is the continuing criminalisation of migration and migrants which fosters a culture of distrust between EU Member States and migrants. Cholewinski commented that '*to a certain degree this culture of distrust has been generated and then reinforced by the developing EU migration law and policy, particularly in the adoption of measures that stigmatise migrants, in the absence of a more principled approach based on detailed human rights guarantees.*' (Cholewinski, 2007). We consider the specific issues around criminalisation and stigmatisation below. However, as the quotation above also points to the third and fundamental flaw in the legal framework, which is the absence of human rights consideration in the law and policy in this area. Because there is no coherence, no basis from which migration policy can start to build a framework and because much of the law and policy specifically tackling irregular migration criminalises migration processes and outcomes, human rights considerations and protections are not mainstreamed throughout and can therefore get lost. In fact human rights considerations appear, at best, an afterthought in the legislation and we consider this in more detail below. In the latter part of the paper we consider whether more recent provisions have taken a more human rights based approach and to what extent we need to continue to strive for law and policy on migration which builds a coherent framework from a human rights base.

Lack of Coherence

In this paper we have briefly described three key areas of law and policy which relate to irregular migration and even just considering those areas highlights that there is no coherent framework or even base line from which to deal with migration into and across the EU. This situation is exacerbated when considering other areas of migration policy such as the regulation of labour market access for TCNs or the free movement of persons as it applies to EU citizens. In short, there is no migration policy overall in the EU. Instead the EU provisions focus on specific issues as they arise in relation to migration and thus do not take a holistic approach which sees migrants as human beings to whom human rights apply. Dover notes that '*the EU has found itself in a pernicious position whereby economic logic dictates that a supply of economic migrants is necessary to ensure that the EU continues to grow economically, but this is counter-balanced by a social and political resistance to migrants*' (Dover, 2008).

While migration policy must be multifaceted and address issues arising out of many different circumstances, it must also be internally coherent in order to be effective. Tensions and contradictions within the policies and legal provisions undermine the regulation of migration, making it more difficult to protect the interests of migrants, third countries and EU Member States.

In this regards, we can highlight that some steps have been taken to harmonise the different aspects of EU migration policy in 2008. Indeed, the EU adopted its "Global Approach to Migration and Mobility" (GAMM) (European Commission, 2011) to unite all migration-related policies in a coherent manner. The overall goal of the GAMM was to encourage regular migration and to fight irregular migration through cooperation with third countries (both those from which migrants originate and those through which they transit), including by concluding "mobility partnerships". Nonetheless, the implementation of the GAMM has proved difficult and the EU's approach to migration has often been dominated by an excessively security-oriented approach.

Therefore, contradictions and tensions are what we find when considering the legal provisions discussed above.

Criminalisation of Migration

In 2008, Robert Dover argued that "*The EU and its member governments have allowed themselves to fall into a mindset where all migration is seen as inherently undesirable and, in many circumstances, threatening*" (Dover, 2008). This negative approach to migration and immigrants in particular is evident in the legal measures governing this area. Despite a change in the use of language in academic and some policy circles, much of the official documentation still refers to illegal rather than for example irregular migration and little effort is made to clarify that the irregular migrants themselves are not criminals merely because of their irregular status in a Member State (Atikon, 2006, Hammerberg, 2009).

The efforts of the ECJ in particular is to assert non-criminal status of irregular migrants in line with the law and policy which stress migrants' inviolable rights; but that is contradicted by the legislative measures and policy documents, which are at the same time introducing provisions that stigmatize migration and migrants. The European Union aims to facilitate the development of regular migration and to ensure the economic growth of the EU and thus has established several rules to facilitate the entry of highly skilled migrants in their studies and in the workplace (Block, 2012). However this does not allow for a consideration of immigrants who come from countries in which there is a total or near lack of adequate education and possibility of work, which are the very reason why they decide to migrate to the EU. The migrants do not have the necessary requirements to enter as regular and therefore enter through irregular channels. This creates a policy which distinguishes the immigrants into different categories, assigning different rights and protections. Anyone who has not entered the country through a regular channel and has been subjected to the relevant checks at border control has entered illegally but that does not mean that they are criminals.

The criminalisation and stigmatisation of migrants is perhaps most obvious in relation to the provisions of human trafficking (Duvell et al, 2010). Even though, those being trafficked do not themselves commit a criminal offence in EU law, they are surrounded by a web of criminality. The people transporting them into the EU, providing access to migration channels and employing them in an EU member state commit criminal offences. Even where the irregular migrant can regularise their status following arrival, they cannot do so where they maintain contact with their traffickers. So, in many cases, the migrants themselves are treated as criminals. The language used in the policy and legal documents as well as by popular media in member states does little to highlight that the migrants themselves are not in fact criminals. Language such as '*combating illegal migration*', or "*fighting the influx of illegal migrants*" rather suggest that we should see the migrants as criminals, not as human beings. For that reason, the social sciences to avoid any discriminatory connotation, prefer to refer to "*undocumented*" or "*irregular*" migrants (Triandafyllidou, 2010).

Where are the human rights?

The lack of coherence taken together with the increasing criminalisation of migrants and migration mean that questions of human rights have been side-lined in the debate at policy level (Carens, 2008). In fact, it can be argued that human rights instruments side-line migrants in many ways (Ambrosini, 2013, Denbour and Kelly, 2011, Mann, 2013).

Kengerlinsky wrote "*A human being with his or her interests is central to the EU, and the Member States have a responsibility to protect the human rights of all those within their territory and jurisdiction. There is an individual and collective duty of EU States to protect persons moving across borders and it is incumbent on them to act and co-operate to achieve this purpose* " (Kengerlinsky, 2007). The Europe Union does not seem to really want to implement these protections towards irregular immigrants.

A confirmation of these considerations, for instance, are some provisions of the Directive 2008/115/EC, also called Return Directive. A provision among all is that which seems not to consider the fundamental rights of foreigners subject to expulsion: the Article 13, indeed, provides the opportunity for the stranger to obtain judicial suspension of the decision to return, which is only considered as a possibility and not as an automatic effect resulting to the proposition of the appeal. In this way, the immigrant who decides to contest the decision concerning him or her, may do so in vain, because once the expulsion has been done a possible ruling in favour, from the authority Court, would be, as said, *inutiliter data*.

Moreover, it must be emphasized that it is in contradiction with the jurisprudence of the European Court of Human Rights, which requires the suspension whenever there is a risk to the stranger of torture or inhuman and degrading treatments, but the Directive does not seem to regard this principle (Winkler, 2011).

The lack protection of human rights is also demonstrated by the constant maintenance, in many aspects of the matter, of the *domestic jurisdiction*, which does not allow to the European Union to have a social policy and legislation that is unique and responds to strict rules (McNamara, 2013). Indeed the European Union continues, consciously, to limit itself to sanction general principles which, in most cases, are applied differently in most States. This manifests that the will does not want to really protect immigrants, especially the irregulars, thus demonstrating to consider the illegal immigrants only in the sense of problems, revealing in part a culture of distrust towards that matter and leaving the solution of this phenomenon to the discretion of each Member Country.

The new legal framework: addressing the problems?

The question, subsequently to the analysis conducted, is how to address the problem of a major and effective protection of human rights of irregular immigrants? (See also Vasta, 2011). We have to highlight that some improvements have been introduced in the last years.

For instance, we could begin stressing the Return Directive mentioned above. Although on the one hand, there are several provisions that are do not protect human rights, other provisions have been included: the right of foreigners to receive free legal advice[5]; the requirement to state the reasons in fact and in law of return decisions; the introduction of a ban on holding the migrant in prison throughout the process. There is therefore a much clearer articulation that the migrant does not have to be considered a criminal.

In regards to this Directive, throughout a communication on the EU's Return Policy adopted by the European Commission on 28 March 2014, which stressed the need for better practical implementation of the EU Return Directive and of return policies in general, the EU highlights that the full respect for fundamental rights has to be ensured within return procedures and states the intention of adopting, within one year, a "*Return Handbook*", containing common guidelines, best practices and recommendations to member states for carrying out returns in a manner consistent with relevant international standards, and in line with the safeguards established within the Return Directive. The assessment also includes comparative country information on detention, including alternatives to detention, monitoring of forced return and suspensive effects of an appeal against removal directions.

Case law has also helped to clarify the position. Saadi v UK (2008) makes clear that there must be a nexus between the purpose of the procedure and its duration, therefore detention can go on only until the need of expulsion. In Amuur v France (1996) the Court noted that the location and conditions of detention must be appropriate in light of the fact that detention does not apply to an individual criminal but a migrant.

Another positive measure was recently introduced: when the European Parliament adopted the Regulation establishing rules of surveillance in FRONTEX through coordinated joint operation, already mentioned. The European Parliament Committee on Civil Liberties, Justice and Home Affairs (LIBE) on 20 February 2014 voted in support of the compromise text on the regulation. The rules required units participating in FRONTEX operations to ensure the safety and human dignity of intercepted or rescued persons including an obligation to identify vulnerable persons such as victims of

[5] In this case, however, has not been expected, in a system in which free legal advice and assistance provided only on request, that the stranger was informed of this possibility and in a language that they can understand.

trafficking and unaccompanied migrant children and provide them with adequate assistance[6]. This seems to be an attempt to pay mayor attention to the protection of human rights.

Some relevant improvements are also detectable in the new EU directive on human trafficking, mentioned before, implemented in April 2013. Some researchers have stressed that it is a much more substantial document than its predecessor, reflecting the growing concern among Member States regarding the development of the phenomenon of trafficking in human beings. Indeed it takes an integrated, holistic, and human rights approach to the issue, building on the pre-existing legal frameworks provided by the UN, the International Labour Organisation (ILO), the Council of Europe, and the EU Charter of Fundamental Rights.

The new EU Directive referred to above is Directive 2011/36/EU on Preventing and Combating Trafficking in Human Beings and Protecting its Victims. The Directive replaces the Framework Decision discussed above and seems to take a different approach, focusing more on protecting victims and having more obvious regard for Human Rights. In this section, we examine the Directive to see the extent to which it might address some of the concerns we identified earlier.

The Directive does focus more on human rights than previous legislation in this area. It explicitly refers to European and International human rights' instruments. More importantly, it also specifies some of the tools critical to the application of the provisions and outlines of some measures to support the effectiveness of protection of the rights in question. In fact, the Directive adopts a more comprehensive approach, which is no longer confined to the fight against organised crime but aimed at ensuring greater protection of victims. This can be seen in the title of the Directive itself but is made explicit in reference to "position of vulnerability" in Article 2 (2), and the explicit non-criminalization of the trafficked persons for any offences arising from having been trafficked. The conceptualisation of trafficking has been broadened to include activities into which trafficked migrants might be forced on arrival in

---

[6] FRONTEX reported that the number of irregular entries to the EU almost doubled in the third quarter of 2013 compared to the same period in the previous year.

the host state to engage in activities such as begging, shoplifting, drug dealing or prostitution. A broadening of our understanding of trafficking and exploitation allows for a more holistic approach to dealing with the issues arising. Other provisions are also to be welcomed. For example, judges have the power to use the means of the seizure, confiscation of proceeds of crime to fund assistance and protection of victims; and the Directive promotes civil society organizations, including NGOs: Member States must work closely with them, especially with regards to policy initiatives, information campaigns and awareness programs, research and education and training, and verification and evaluation of the impact of anti-trafficking measures.

While the change in the law is to be welcomed, it must be remembered that much of the provisions may be very difficult to enforce in practice because of the victims' vulnerable situation. The power many traffickers hold over their victims, the lack of funding for NGOs and other organisations trying to offer support. In particular, the right to compensation may turn out to be symbolic rather than anything else (see work done by the compact project). Furthermore, the criminal law elements of migration policy remain in this area. While criminal sanctions have been imposed against those responsible for trafficking is not criticized, care must be taken that such sanctions do not impact negatively on those being trafficked. An increase in minimum criminal sanctions and provisions aimed at facilitating prosecutions are welcomed as they may act as a deterrent and may help cases to be brought to conclusion even where victims retract statements or are unable to cooperate.

Obviously, it is necessary to see how this Directive will be implemented and applied by each individual Member State, whereby the majority seem to have had difficulty complying with European standards in this area (see CEDU Siliadin v France 2005). While progress has been made, there are still underdeveloped aspects and much will depend on implementation and the willingness of Member States to cooperate with each other.

Another important point is the increase of irregular entrance of immigrants who reach the coasts of South European Member State to enter in EU, by the Mediterranean Sea. Indeed, many more illegal border crossings in the Mediterranean were detected in 2013 than in 2012, even more than during the 2011 Arab Spring[7].

The irregular immigrants arrive by boats guided by traffickers and a lot of them lost their lives at sea. After the Lampedusa tragedy, on October 2013, the EU's objective according to Commissioner's Cecilia Malmstrom, was to avoid any more loss of life by identifying and rescuing vessels at risk and thereby reinforcing the humanitarian elements of EU border security policies. The European Commission in a Communication of December 2013 (European Commission 2013) on the work of Mediterranean Task Force, underlined that all the actions proposed by the Task Force "*will have to be fully compliant with international human rights standards*".

The Mediterranean Task Force also calls for cooperation with national authorities that have already undertaken such operations, Operations as Mare Nostrum launched by the Italian Defence Ministry after the Lampedusa tragedy and covered a wide area arriving close to the Libyan coast (Italian Ministry of Defence, 2014), Given the difficulties that Italy had in managing the high monthly costs of operations and the huge number of migrants, the Italian Government asked for a significant aid to the EU. Afterwards, on November 1, 2014, Joint Operation Triton has been started by Frontex (see www.fronte.europa.eu). It will cover the maritime area close the European borders with a budget estimated at 2.9 million per month. EU Member States should contribute with the necessary equipment to support the Italian authorities. The focus of Joint Operation Triton will be primarily border management with the consequence of a lack of a joint rescue operation at European level. Despite the intents showed by the EU, it is necessary to highlight that the measures adopted do not seem to be effective and are in contradiction with the EU policy expressed on the issue. [8]

---

[7] In 2012, trans-Mediterranean irregular migrants accounted for 80.6% of the total number of irregular migrants counted along the EU external borders. In the third quarter of 2013, the most common nationality of intercepted migrants was Syrian.

[8] It is necessary stressed a recent prevision of EU: in the conclusion of European Council on 26 to 27 June 2014 in Brussels, the Council agreed the strategic guidelines for legislative and operational planning in the area of freedom, security and justice for the next five years. The European Council Conclusions stressed that one of the key priorities should be to consistently transpose, effectively implement and consolidate the legal instruments and policy measures already in place. The Council highlighted that the treaty principles of

What's the alternative?

So what is the alternative? In our view, European migration policy must place human rights at the centre of its considerations. It must build a coherent framework that governs migration at all levels and in all contexts and does not privilege certain migrants over others (El-Enav, 2013). Beginning with human rights as the basis of such a policy would value all migrants and the potential contribution they can make to Member States and the EU overall. It would encourage Member States to treat all migrants including irregular ones with far more respect than is currently shown and would help ensure that processes for regulating borders and enforcing that regulation are set out in a way which preserves human dignity. This approach requires a clearer and systematic European legal framework on the matter of migration generally (Miller, 2008).

To create a legal framework in the field of EU migration which includes a stronger protection of human rights of irregular migrants, first of all, it is necessary to encourage a more effective way of thinking about how the problems leading to irregular migration can be addressed in order to alleviate the push factors causing migrants to choose irregular status over staying in their home countries. This might include a rethinking of EU external relations and the giving of aid to third countries.

Moreover, the use of Mobility Partnership (Healther, 2013) and Bilateral Agreements, to encourage effective collaboration among the countries of origin and the EU and Member States should be adopted. Seemingly successful examples include the Mobility Partnership in

solidarity and fair sharing of responsibility, in accordance with Article 80 of the Treaty on the Functioning of the European Union (TFEU), should guide Member States and the EU towards an efficient and well-managed migration, asylum and borders policy. The Council also called for the development of strategies to maximize the opportunities and regular channels for people to migrate to Europe, while "tackling irregular migration resolutely". Other priorities identified by the Council include: strengthening active integration policies and social cohesion, addressing smuggling and trafficking in human beings more efficiently, establishing an effective common return policy and enforce readmission agreements and reinforcing Frontex's operational assistance, including the possibility of creating a new "European system of border guards". Meanwhile, Maltese Prime Minister Joseph Muscat welcomed the conclusions statement to share responsibility of irregular migration flows. Governments of the EU's member states at the southern border had repeatedly called on the EU to share responsibility for large numbers of migrant arrivals.

2013 with Morocco and more recently, in 2014 with Tunisia. Mobility Partnership established with neighbourhood countries offer concrete frameworks for dialogue and cooperation on migration issues, reinforcing capabilities and encouraging coherence in the internal governance of migration. The overall aims of these partnerships are to facilitate and organize legal migration (for citizens of the partner countries) and to strengthen measures addressing irregular migration (for the citizens of the partner countries and transiting migrants) while respecting human rights. These partnerships are selective and are concluded with third countries only once certain conditions, such as cooperation on irregular migration and the existence of effective mechanisms for re-admission, are met. However this last point emphasises that partnerships are EU-centred and that the contours of the EU's external dimensions of migration policy continue to be primarily insecurity, immobility and conditionality driven, meanwhile the attention should be directed towards the aims of supporting economic and political reform. Moreover, more efforts should be made to improve and enhance in a practical way the possibilities of regular channels for migration (Wiesbrock, 2010).

Conclusions

In this paper we have outlined some of the current EU laws and policy in irregular migration to highlight the lack of a consistent framework in this area and to show how the continuing criminalisation of migration leads to irregular migrants being left in difficult situations without much human rights based protection. We have argued that recent legal changes have improved matters a little, by recognising the importance of migrants' basic human rights particularly in relation to trafficking. However, our overall conclusion must be that we are not there yet and that in order to create an environment where the potential of migrants can be realised for their benefit and the benefit of their host countries, we need to reconceptualise EU level migration policy based on a human rights framework.

Legislation and Case law referred to:

Regulation EC No. 2007/2004 of 26 October 2004, O.J.L. 349, 25 November 2004, p.1-11.
Regulation EC No. 562/2006 of 15 March 2006, O.J.L. 105, 13 April 2006, p. 1-32.
Regulation EC No 810/2009 of 13 July 2009, O.J.L. 243, 15 September 2009, p.1-58.

Directive 2001/51/EU of 28 June 2001, O.J.L. 187, 10 July 2001, p. 45-46.
Directive 2004/82/EC, of 29 April 2004, O.J.L. 261, 6 August 2004, p.24-27.
Directive 2011/36/EU of 5 April 2011, O.J.L., 15 April 2011, p.1.
Directive 2009/52/EC of 18 June 2009, O.J.L. 168, 30 June 2009, p. 24-32.
Directive 2004/81/EC, 29 April 2004, O.J.L. 261, 6 August 2004, p. 3-3.
Directive 2002/90/EC of 28 November 2002, O.J.L. 328, 5 December 2002, p. 17-18.

Saadi versus United Kindom. European Court of Human Rights of 29 Juanuary 2008, appeal No. 13229/03.
Amuur versus France, in Reports, III, 1996. European Court of Human Rights of 24 June 1996, appeal No. 19776/92.

Chapter 2: The Making of Immigration Policies in Turkey: An analysis of the Law on Foreigners and International Protection Drafting Process

Deniz Eroğlu

Although Turkey has been an important immigration and asylum country (see Kale, 2005; Kaya, 2009, 2012; Kirisci, 1996, 2002, 2003, 2007) as well as a transit county (Sahin-Mencutek, 2012) in the region, the legal infrastructure to deal with the migration subject has been somewhat poor . This field has been governed by piecemeal legislations, and this lack of primary legislation, which covers both rights and responsibilities has been indicated as one of the reasons for decreasing the level of protection given to refugees and asylum seekers (Amnesty International, 2009). When we come to 2011, it is possible to see a remarkable development in the field of asylum seekers, although negotiations with the EU remained in deadlock. In 2011, The Law on Foreigners and International Protection in Turkey *(No. 6458)* was drafted and it was approved by Parliament on 4 April 2013.[1] This was an innovative movement in the history of Turkish migration policies because it was the first comprehensive law to cover both foreigners and those who need international protection.

While this law constitutes a milestone in the field of migration in Turkey, the drafting process is equally important. The process of drafting the law was very unusual by Turkish standards, since it was a transparent process that involved different actors (Kirisci, 2012, p. 63). Taking this into account, this article has set out to scrutinize the process of drafting Turkey's first ever asylum and migration law. To this end, it analyses the role of bureaucracy and explores how a new institution dealing with migration has brought a new era for immigration policy-making in Turkey. Based on interview data that consist of several elites from different institutions within the policy-making mechanism, bureaucracy, the author argues, is an important

[1] The Official Gazette of the Republic Of Turkey No.28615 11.04.2013. Law on Foreigners and International Protection No.6458.

institution in the immigration policy-making in Turkey, therefore a change in the key agency dealing with migration, mainly transformation from police centered decision-making to civil bureaucracy, has introduced a new era, which incorporates different actors to the immigration policy-making.

The rest of the article is organized as follows. The first part provides the theoretical background of the analysis. The second part details the importance of the bureaucratic elite in immigration policy-making, and it describes the recent institutional changes in this field of policy-making in Turkey. The third part explores the analysis of the drafting process of the Law on Foreigners and International Protection in Turkey.

Theoretical Background

Several studies in the field of migration focus on immigration policy-making, in order to examine immigration policies. Geddes is one such pioneer, who emphasized policy-making and maintains that "*we need to analyse the form that immigration politics takes and the institutional venues where decisions were made*" (Geddes, 2003, p.21). In line with Geddes, Selm (2005) focuses on the domestic institutional context of policy decision-making and planning, mainly the administrative organs of states, in his study for the Global Commission on International Migration. After examining the institutional configuration of several different countries, namely Canada, Australia, Denmark, the Netherlands, Sweden, the United Kingdom, the United States, Georgia, South Africa, the Philippines and Mexico, she argues that domestic politics and policy institutions can have interests in immigration related topics (Selm, 2005, p.10). Her research is important, since it reveals where migration policy is formulated, it has implications regarding the 'image' and 'perception'. She argues that '*how any country manages migration would appear at first sight to be less about its migration concerns per se, and more about the cultural, political and economic decisions that have been taken historically about national institutions and their relationship with and understanding of migration matters'* (Selm, 2005, p.10).While Selm (2005) draws attention to the role of the institutional context, to help in the understanding of migration in relevant countries, Rosenhek suggests that '*the position of different state agencies within the institutional structure affects their preference formation*' (Rosenhek, 2000,p. 53). Rosenhek's research contributes to the literature by indicating the 'dynamic' feature of the institutional setting and policy-making rather than approaching these concepts as static structures. This study maintains that new agendas and interests developed by agencies, as well as intra-state tensions among different institutions, shape policy formation and implementation (Rosenhek, 2000, p.50).

While scholars investigate the state institutions in migration policy-making, they particularly highlight the bureaucracy. Taras (2012) defines immigration policy as being under both bureaucratic and political control. According to the author, immigration policy can be highly politicized but it has also a technical side which "*bureaucrats are better equipped to manage*" (Taras, 2012, p.9). He investigates the role of bureaucrats in determining immigration policy choice. He contributes to the literature by adding officials' ideas as factors in influencing policies and argues that bureaucrats' own judgments regarding immigration influence immigration policy outcomes.

Calavita takes a step further by highlighting "agent" factors within the institutions. Her research challenges studies that treat the state as "monolithic" and shows the importance of examining "specific state agencies, institutions and cadres of state managers" (Calavita, 2010, p.190). Her dialectical-structural account of immigration policy examination indicates the importance of 'human agency' working in state institutions, and she concludes that:

One thing is certain. Structures don't act, people do. If we are to progress beyond the current impasse in state theory, we must bridge the methodological and analytical divides that have limited our theoretical vision, and incorporate our analysis both social structure and political actors who are situated within those structures (Calavita, 2010, p.198).

As literature rightly indicates, who deals with migration question in countries is an important factor to further an understanding for policies. Following on from the literature, this article is devoted to examining the drafting process of the Law on Foreigners and international Protection in Turkey by approaching it from a policy-making perspective.

Decision-making regarding immigration policies: transformation from police-centred decision-making to civil bureaucracy

The influence of bureaucratic elites' power in the decision-making process varies from one country to another. In the Turkish context, we see a considerably important role of this institution in affecting policy-making process although its role and relation to the political elite have undergone significant changes over time.

Fisek states that *'[b]ureaucracy, i.e. the performance of government activity through the agencies of permanent and privileged officials, is one of Turkey's more firmly entrenched institutions'* (Fisek, 1982 , p.120-121).

The bureaucracy plays an essential role in the policy-making mechanism and is not solely an institution to implement policies. To be sure in democratic countries, the executive bureaucracy is expected to work under the direction of the politicians. In Turkey, however, appointed officials have very high levels of authority, which sometimes makes them more influential than politicians on public policies (Cevik & Demirci, 2008, p.37).

Despite Turkey's modernizing goals, the bureaucracy has continued to play an important role in political decision-making. Owing to Turkey's statist tradition, the status and power of its bureaucracy is greater than in modern democratic countries. This is perhaps the most important feature of the Turkish bureaucracy. The bureaucracy's strength has contributed to imbalance and created instability in the political system by forcing power to be shared between politicians and bureaucrats. Thus, bureaucrats have significance in the political system (Durgun & Yayman, 2005, p.105)

In order to understand Turkish bureaucrats' position in policy-making and their significant role in Turkish political life, scholars usually turn to the country's historical background in order to set the scene for "*the autonomy of the bureaucracy*" in the Turkish political system. (Durgun, 2002; Eryilmaz, 2010; Heper, 1976, 2010; Pustu, 2007; Yalcindag, 1970). They maintain that the bureaucratic tradition of the Ottoman Empire had implications for the Turkish political system, and the bureaucratic cadre has had a remarkable influence on the political life of the Republic. The Turkish Republic, according to Özbudun, '*inherited from the Ottoman Empire a strong and centralized, highly bureaucratic state in which rational- legal bureaucratic norms prevail*' (Özbudun, 2000, p.7). Starting from the early years of the Republic, bureaucracy was a very important part of the decision-making process in Turkish politics. However, its role, efficiency and connection to political elites have changed throughout history.

The power and autonomy of the bureaucracy diminished after the 1950s and was politicized after the 1970s and became closer to the ruling party from 2002. However, scholars still underline the importance of bureaucracy in certain public policy areas (e.g.Cevik & Demirci, 2008; Robins, 2009). What is also clear is that the EU negotiation process has loaded new duties onto bureaucratic elites, reinforcing their importance in policy-making. Those policy areas in which parties show little interest and those fields that are related to EU membership are those where the bureaucratic elite still have great influence.

When it comes to immigration policies, the traditional role of the bureaucracy in public policy-making is not the only reason for analysing the role of this institution in policies. It needs to be examined because other actors, politicians and civil societies have showed very little interest in this topic until recently and the bureaucratic elite remained dominant actors in the field. Moreover, the EU accession negotiation process assigned new tasks to the bureaucratic elites, since immigration and asylum issues fall into Chapter 24 of the EU *Acquis* that Turkey has to adopt. Taken together, bureaucratic elites – '*men [and women] behind big desks*' (Schneider, 1992) – are important for this study.

Immigration and asylum have been dealt with at state level for a long time. The 1934 Law on Settlement (No: 2510) provided for a strong state role in immigration decision-making. Article 3 of this law expresses that only those of 'Turkish descent and culture' can attain refugee status. It authorised the Council of Ministers to decide who had a Turkish descent and culture by stating that '*[w]hat individuals and the peoples of what countries are considered attached to Turkish culture shall be determined by a decision of the Council of Minister'.*[2]

Before changes were made to the size and the nature of immigration in Turkey, the asylum issue was mainly the responsibility of the Foreigners Department within the General Directorate of Security of the Interior, with the cooperation of the Foreign Ministry and the UNHCR. During the Cold War era, the Foreigners Department within the General Directorate of Security of the Interior Ministry and the Ministry of Foreign Affairs cooperated with the UNHCR, in order to deal with the asylum question (Kirisci, 2004a, p. 4). Until the mid-1980s, very close cooperation took place between the UNHCR and the Turkish government, whereby the UNHCR took a role in determining refugee status for both European and non-European refugees (Biehl, 2009; Kirisci, 2001; Zieck, 2010).

Due to change in the size and composition of new migration movements in the late 1980s and early 1990s, The Turkish government needed to introduce its first national legislation related to the asylum question, entitled '*The Regulation on the Procedures and the Principles Related to Mass Influx and Foreigners Arriving in Turkey either as Individuals or in Groups Wishing to Seek Asylum either from Turkey or Requesting Residence Permits with the Intention of Seeking Asylum from a Third Country*' (November, 1994).[3] The regulation was the primary source of legislation (together with The Circular No: 57) dealing with the asylum issue in Turkey until the Law on Foreigners and International protection No. 6458 was adopted, although some of its Articles were amended and additional circulars issued.[4]

---

[2] The Official Gazette of the Republic Of Turkey No. 2733 21.06.1934. Law on Settlement No.2510. Also See The Official Gazette of The Republic Of Turkey No. 3162 21.11.1935. Law on Amendment of Some Articles of the Law on Settlement No.2848.

[3] The Official Gazette of the Republic Of Turkey No.22127 30.11.1994. The 1994 Regulation on Procedures and Principles related to Mass Influx and Foreigners Arriving in Turkey either as Individuals or in Groups Wishing to Seek Asylum Either from Turkey or Requesting Residence Permits with the Intension of Seeking Asylum from a Third Country (No.94/6169).

[4] The Republic of Turkey Ministry of Interior Circular No.57 22.06.2006. The Implementation Directive to the 1994 Regulation.

The conditions that attracted the attention of state authorities to the asylum issue in the 1990s, and the 1994 Regulation itself, are important in developing an understanding of the actors dealing with this issue. The 1994 Regulation was concluded by taking into account the mass refugee influxes, which Turkey experienced after the Iran-Iraq War (1980-1988) and the Gulf War (1990-1991). As a result, security concerns were clearly reflected in the legislation (Baklacioglu, 2009; Biehl, 2009; Kirisci, 2004b). This regulation was prepared by officials from the Ministry of the Interior and only the Ministry of Foreign Affairs was consulted, while this regulation was drafted (Kirisci, 1996, p.301). In other words, there was strong centralization of power and the role of bureaucracy in the decision-making process pertaining to migration at that time. Given the concerns over national security at the time, this bureaucratic supremacy is not surprising.

When the importance of the refugee issue for Turkey decreased, relations with the UNHCR normalized. However, the Department of Foreigners, Borders and Asylum of the General Directorate of Security within the Turkish National Police of the Ministry of the Interior (TNP) remained a major institution in the field as a result of their security-related perspective. Furthermore, as time went by, the role of this state institution increased and the police force started to act more as a decision-maker on asylum issues. Subsequent circulars increased the role of the TNP. Baklacioglu argues "*[...] in cases where important decisions about the destiny and rights of the refugees appear captured within the personal attributes and personal degree of tolerance of the police officers in the Foreigners Departments of MOI or respectively in the Governorship*" (Baklacioglu, 2009, p.109).

The TNP has been the main and most influential agency with which an asylum seeker must have contact after entering the territory and until their resettlement in a third country. In addition to a direct role in the asylum process, police officers of the General Directorate of Security also participate in policy decision-making mechanisms at state level. '*The TNP is the only decision-maker in individual cases. In the matter of deciding policies, it is one of the significant components of the policy making process*' (interview 1). This was not only the result of a lack of legislation, but also of the long-standing indifference of political authorities to the subject. Until recently, the government responded to the immigration issue with ad hoc decisions whenever mass refugee influxes occurred. The strong position of the TNP in the immigration field has drawn abundant criticism from bureaucratic elites as well as NGO representatives (interviews 2, 3, 4).

The EU negotiation process was a remarkable turning point for Turkish authorities. They had to confront the reality that Turkey was an important transit and destination country and needs durable and institutionalized solutions on immigration (interview 5). The negotiation also paved the way for policy diversifications and increased the number of actors dealing with the issue. The most important institutional transformation in this policy area was undoubtedly, the emergence of a new institution, the Bureau on Development and Implementation of the Legislation on Asylum and Migration and Administrative Capacity (henceforth referred to as the Asylum and Migration Bureau), in October 2008. Here, it is important to stress that the responsible bureaucratic organ is still the MOI, since the new agency was established under the auspices of this ministry. The new bureaucratic elites working for the Asylum and Migration Bureau started to take on immigration policy tasks. This affected the position of TNP officers "*who [had] been in their positions for decades, and were resistant to changes*" (Tolay, 2012, p.135). This institution aimed to create the necessary legislative and administrative structures to support the adoption of the EU *Acquis*, to carry out EU projects regarding this matter and to inform the Undersecretary of the MOI about developments (Ministry of Interior Asylum and Migration Bureau, n.d.). Although this administrative body paved the way for a new process for the Turkish immigration policy-making mechanism, there is still an important role for TNP in the system. TNP and bureaucrats work together at the new agency to determine Turkish asylum policies and to implement the reforms necessary for EU membership.

Currently, the MOI takes leading roles in the field of immigration in Turkey. However, there are other institutions that also make decisions when immigration policies are decided upon. The Ministry of Foreign Affairs has traditionally been a significant institution that has had responsibility for migration issues in Turkey. Tolay maintains that while '*the Ministry of Foreign Affairs had the most leverage on migration issues in the 1990s, it is now the Ministry of the Interior that carries most responsibility'* (Tolay, 2012, p. 135). The 2006 amendments to the 1994 Regulation removed the necessity to ask the opinion of other ministries, although the Foreign Ministry remains important because the policy has obvious implications for international relations. The migration issue is related to the state's relations with other countries, so the Ministry of Foreign Affairs is thus intrinsically part of the process. The opening of the accession negotiation process between Turkey and the EU has had a particular influence on strengthening the role of this ministry, because the immigration topic is one of the subjects on the negotiation table. Although the core role of the Ministry of Foreign Affairs has gradually decreased over the course of time, it still faces some key tasks since immigration and asylum are significant topics in accession negotiations with the EU. In addition, The Ministry of Foreign Affairs played a vital role while the Law on Foreigners and International Protection was drafted as an officer from this institution describes (interview 2).

All in all, the Turkish bureaucracy, particularly the Ministry of the Interior, is a very important political institution in the field of migration in Turkey. Therefore a change in the key agency dealing with migration has affected the process of drafting the Law on Foreigners and International Protection.

An unusual policy-making process: drafting the law on foreigners and international protection

The process for filling the gaps in the Turkish asylum system was mentioned by underlining the legislative and institutional requirements necessary for migration management in the Turkish National Action Plan for the Adoption of the EU *Acquis* in asylum and migration in 2005. Furthermore, several progress reports emphasized institutional and legislative needs in relation to asylum.

However, the bureaucratic elite do not regard the EU as the only motivation for initiating the process of law-making. They also underline the importance of a legal loophole in the Turkish asylum system. According to the officers in the Asylum and Migration Bureau, Turkey needs to develop a unique system for itself by considering the increase in the number of immigrants that come to this country, apart from external actors (interview 6). NGO representatives also agree with this. According to the representative of the Multeci-Der, is that not every development is done just because 'the EU wants this'. Nowadays, Turkey-EU relations have frozen and no new chapters from *Acquis* have been opened for negotiations. There is no enthusiasm to gain EU membership, whereas this desire used to be strong in Turkey. However, there are still ongoing endeavours to improve the system *(interview 8).*

In line with this notion, the General Reasons document was published by the Bureau to provide a rationale for this law. This document highlights the changing nature of Turkey from a 'transit country' to a 'target country' for different types of immigrants. In line with this notion, the General Reasons document was published by the Bureau to provide a rationale for this law. This document highlights the changing nature of Turkey from a 'transit country' to a 'target country' for different types of immigrants. As the document clearly points out, there has been a considerable change in the number of immigrants arriving in Turkey since the 1990s. Nonetheless, current Turkish legislation regarding foreigners dates back to the 1950s and does not satisfy today's requirements. The legal loophole with respect to asylum and refugees is particularly highlighted in the Reasons Document. The document also highlights Chapter 24 of the *Acquis Communautaire*, in which immigration and asylum are embedded in gaining EU membership. This chapter includes necessary measures and investment projects in order to finalise legal regulations, administrative structuring and physical infrastructure projects to align Turkish migration policies (The General Directorate of Laws and Decrees, 2012).

After its establishment, this Bureau became the leading agency dealing with immigration issues. Beginning on 9 February 2009, meetings of the Task Force for the Asylum-Migration Action Plan began to be held under the coordination of this agency. Bureaucratic elites initiated the process of drafting the Law on Foreigners and International Protection on 15 June 2009. The UNHCR and the IOM approved providing technical assistance. Originally, the Law on Asylum and the Law on Foreigners were planned as two different decrees, so two separate but interconnected units dealt with the process. The asylum unit started its studies on 1 September 2009, while studies for the Law on Foreigners started three days after this date. The bureaucratic elite were particularly keen to include every actor in the process while the process for these laws was initiated. They tried to understand the field and the subject. Then they constituted a core cadre, consisting of people from the Prime Ministry and academics. They also invited experts from the UNHCR and IOM to submit their opinions while the Articles were being designed. Furthermore, these Articles were sent to NGOs in order to prepare them for the new process. They also twice consulted with the ECtHR and the European Commission and skimmed ECtHR decisions. Considering the decisions of the ECtHR was sine qua non rule for them. *(*interviews 6, 7,9*)*.

It is important to underline that the new regime realised that it was necessary to take NGOs' opinions into consideration while formulating new policies. They expect to see NGOs in the policy-making process, while immigration and asylum policies are determined. For that reason, the bureaucratic elite aims to institutionalize their relationship with the NGOs and keep on cooperating in this policy field. *(*interview 6*)* On 3 March 2010, the Article headings of the draft Law on Asylum and the Law on Foreigners were shared with NGO representatives and academics. On 6 October 2010, NGOs' comments were requested. Subsequently, a workshop was held on 18th and 19th October 2010, which led to the organization of further meetings. On 28 September 2009, the first meeting with the Advisory Committee for the draft law was held. More meetings were conducted with the advisory committee.

Besides internal meetings and workshops, the EU and several international scholars were also consulted during the process of drafting the law. In addition to drafting meetings in Turkey, Turkish bureaucrats visited different EU countries to meet with migration experts and decision-makers in the field. On 18 December 2009, a draft of the Asylum Migration Road Map was sent to the Delegation of the European Commission in Brussels. This delegation sent back comments regarding the road map on 5 March 2010.[5]

[5] This chronology of studies was obtained on 10 September 2012 during the visit of the

After a protracted process, the draft law was released on 25 January 2011. Its submission to the National Assembly however, took more than a year. The General Directorates of Laws and Decrees under the Prime Ministry presented the draft to the Turkish Parliament on 3 May 2012, and discussions over it at the Plenary Committee began on 20 March 2013. Although the law was released in 2011, it took a long time to arrive on the agenda of the Assembly, largely because of the extraordinary developments on the border between Syria and Turkey. After internal conflict broke out in Syria, thousands of Syrian refugees poured across the border into Turkey. This development shifted attention towards migration. In addition, the Kurdish question pre-occupied the agenda of The Grand National Assembly of Turkey and the Justice and Development Party government began holding meetings with the PKK leadership. Furthermore, between the release of the draft law and its submission to Parliament, some revisions were made to the draft. After the submission to the Plenary Committee, the law was approved by Parliament on 4 April 2013 in order to come into force in 2014.

Conclusion

As a result of interview data gathered from bureaucratic elites dealing with asylum in Turkey, it is clear that the institution of bureaucracy is important in shaping policies in this field. In this regard, changes in the dominant institution in policy-making have been the crucial factor in leading to initiate a new understanding in migration policy-making. Previously, the migration issue was left to the initiative of the security service, which acted as both a decision-maker and implementer. Over time, this policy field has begun to include different institutions and different actors in these institutional settings. The security forces' domination of migration is gradually changing and they are yielding their place to new institutions. The Asylum and Migration Bureau has become the most important institution in the field, and bureaucratic elites in this institution enable other actors to get involved in policy-making. Concrete steps to

Bureau on Development and Implementation of the Legislation on Asylum and Migration and Administrative Capacity.

develop legislation infrastructure in the field of migration were taken by the Asylum and Migration Bureau. For this purpose, this institution drafted Turkey's first ever Law on Foreigners and International Protection, which aims to increase the scope of the rights of asylum seekers and immigrants in Turkey. As shown while explaining the process of law-making, different institutions were consulted and their opinions taken into consideration. Consequently, the Law on Foreigners and International Protection drafting process reveals an inclusive process which is uncommon practice in decision-making on immigration policy matters in Turkey.

Interviews:

As this is analysis part of author's PhD thesis, limited number of interview data was used here. The whole project is based on 52 interviewees. The main interviews were conducted in four cities – Ankara, Izmir, Istanbul and Brussels – and they took place at different time periods in 2011. When the main interviews were undertaken, the Law on Foreigners and International Protection was still a draft. Follow-up interviews were conducted afterwards.

These interviews were conducted in a variety of settings, including elites' offices and meeting rooms of the institutions or organisations. The interview guide consists of semi-structured questions. Interviews were recorded with the participants' consent. Although most of the interviews were tape-recorded, some interviewees, mainly members of the bureaucratic elite, preferred note-taking only. In those situations, repeated questions were asked in order not to miss any important point, and additional meetings were arranged, if necessary. All interviews were transcribed and transcripts of the interviews were analysed qualitatively.

List of Interviews:

TNP officer, Department of Foreigners Borders and Asylum, General Directorate of Security, MOI, 2011.

An officer, Ministry of Foreign Affairs, 2011

An officer, Ministry for EU Affairs, 2011

Amnesty International, Turkey representative

Representative of the Human Rights Joint Platform of Turkey IHOP

An officer, the Asylum and Migration Bureau, 2011

Legal expert

Multeci-Der representative

An officer, Delegation of the European Commission to Turkey

Chapter 3: The principle of non-refoulement a comparative analysis between Turkish national law and international refugee law

Doğa Elçin

Non-refoulement is one of the fundamental principles of international refugee law (Pirjola, 2007:643; Farmer, 2008:5). *Non-refoulement* is not expressed in abstract and general terms, but with specific and clear content (Pirjola, 2007: 639). In the most general sense, *non- refoulement* is a concept which prohibits States from returning a refugee or asylum seeker to territories where there is a risk that his or her life or freedom would be threatened on account of race, religion, nationality, membership of a particular social group, or political opinion (Lauterpacht & Bethlehem, 2003:89).

The principle of *non–refoulement* is closely connected with right to liberty and security within fundamental rights and freedoms. Because of this relevance, Turkish constitutional methodology on fundamental rights and freedoms of foreigners will be followed during this presentation. Both article 16 and the last paragraph of the article 90 make up this constitutional methodology. Article 16 directly regulates foreigner's fundamental rights and freedoms (Taneri, 2012: 233). In accordance with article 16 of the Turkish Constitution[1], *"The fundamental rights and freedoms in respect to aliens may be restricted by law compatible with international law"*.

The last paragraph of article 90 is on conflict between national law and international agreements concerning fundamental rights and freedoms (Taneri, 2012:235). It regulates fundamental rights and freedoms of aliens indirectly. In accordance with the last paragraph of article 90, *"International agreements duly put into effect have the force of law. No appeal to the Constitutional Court shall be made with regard to these agreements, on the grounds that they are unconstitutional. (Sentence added on May 7, 2004; Act No. 5170) In the case of a conflict between international agreements, duly put into*

[1] http://global.tbmm.gov.tr/docs/constitution_en.pdf. (last visited 20.11.2013).

effect, concerning fundamental rights and freedoms and the laws due to differences in provisions on the same matter, the provisions of international agreements shall prevail"[2].

In Turkish national law, the principle of *non-refoulemet* has been regulated for the first time by the Law on Foreigners and International Protection No.6458 in 2014. In this study, the principle of *non-refoulement* will firstly be considered with regards to international conventions that Turkey is a party to because in accordance with article 16 and article 90 of Turkish Constitution, these international conventions have the force of law[3].

Secondly, Turkish national law will be taken into consideration. In this regard, we will begin with Article four of the new Law on Foreigners and International Protection No. 6458. Thereafter article 55/1-a and article 63 will be dealt with.

Lastly, the similarities and differences between Turkish national law and international refugee law will be compared based on the principle of *non-refoulement.*

This presentation is restricted by the legal approach on the principle of *non-refoulement*. The political, social and economic aspects of the principle of *non–refoulement* are out of context. Within the context of the legal approach, extradition and its aspects on criminal law and readmission procedures are excluded because of their comprehensive nature.

International Conventions

1951 Convention relating to the status of refugees

The most significant provision on the principle of *non–refoulemet* is article 33 of the Convention Relating to the Status of Refugees[4]. It

---

[2] http://global.tbmm.gov.tr/docs/constitution_en.pdf. (last visited 20.11.2013).

[3] Within this scope Convention Relating to the Status of Refugees, Convention Against Torture and Other Cruel Inhuman or Degrading Treatment or Punishment, International Covenant on Civil and Political Rights, Geneva Convention Relative to the Protection of Civilian Persons in Time of War, Final Act of the United Nations Conference on the Status of Stateless Persons and Convention for the Protection of Human Rights and Fundamental Freedoms will be examined.

[4] The Convention was signed on 28 July 1951 in Geneva and was entered into force on 22 April 1954. For the original text of the Convention see http://www.unhcr.org/3b66c2aa10.html (last visited: 22.11.2013). Turkey signed the

is because the amount of contracting parties of the convention is significant[5] and developments on international human rights law and international humanitarian law have made interpretation and implementation of this provision dominant (Uzun, 2012:26-7). Paragraph one of article 33 explains the principle of *non-refoulement*. In accordance with Article 33:

"1. No Contracting State shall expel or return (" refouler ") a refugee in any manner whatsoever to the frontiers of territories where his life or freedom would be threatened on account of his race, religion, nationality, membership of a particular social group or political opinion."

In accordance with article 33, the principle of *non- refoulement* comprises not only the individuals who have refugee status but also asylum seekers until they have refugee status (Uzun, 2012). Moreover it does not prevent States from applying the principle of *non-refoulement* even when these people entered into a country illegally (Farmer, 2008:6; Çiçekli, 2009:85; Uzun, 2012:29). The principle of *non-refoulement* is also applied to individuals who have asylum application at the border (Uzun, 2012:31; Stoyanova, 2008:4; Ekşi 2008:2832).

It should be kept in mind that access into States territory or in other words, admission of foreigners, is not an absolute obligation from the point of States (Pirjola, 2007:639; Kabaalioglu & Eksi, 2004:503). However the prerogatives of states to control entrance, residence and deportation of aliens depend on certain human rights obligations (Stoyanova, 2008:2; Pirjola, 2007:639; Kabaalioglu & Eksi, 2004:503). Under this Convention, any act of removal is

---

Convention on 29.08.1951 and has been the party to the Convention by Law No. 359 on 29.08.1961. (Official Gazette: No.10898- 05.09.1961). However, at the time of the ratification of the attendant Protocol Relating to the Status of Refugees in 1968, Turkey opted for the geographical limitation pursuant to Article 1b of the Convention, limiting the scope of the Convention to 'persons who have become refugees as a result of events occurring in Europe. The protocol was signed on 31 January 1967, in New York and was entered into force on 4 October 1967. For the original text of the Protocol see https://treaties.un.org/Pages/ViewDetails.aspx? src=TREATY&mtdsg_no=V-5&chapter=5&lang=en (last visited: 18.12.2013). Council of Ministers Decision 01.07.1968 and no. 6/10266 (Official Gazette: No 12968- 05.08.1968)

[5] 145 States have already been party to the Convention. For the list of parties of the Convention see: http://treaties.un.org/pages/ViewDetailsII.aspx?&src=UNTSONLINE&mtdsg_no=V~2&chapter=5&Temp=mtdsg2&lang=en (last visited: 01.12.2013).

prohibited (Farmer, 2008:5; Çiçekli, 2009:82; Pirjola, 2007:642). The formal description of the act (deportation, expulsion, extradition, return etc.) has no importance (Farmer, 2008:5; Çiçekli, 2009:82; Pirjola, 2007:642). Exemption clause of the principle of *non-refoulement* is regulated in the second paragraph of article 33. It says that:

"The benefit of the present provision may not, however, be claimed by a refugee whom there are reasonable grounds for regarding as a danger to the security of the country in which he is, or who, having been convicted by a final judgement of a particularly serious crime, constitutes a danger to the community of that country."

The uncertainty in the terms of "national security" and "regarding as a danger" are pointed out by doctrine (Farmer, 2008:12; Uzun, 2012:32; Lauterpach & Bethlehem, 2003:90-92). Moreover, Pirjola has noted that under Article 33, paragraph 1 states that concepts central to *non-refoulement* are not generally accepted concepts. In this framework, "persecution", "torture", "cruel", "inhuman and degrading treatment" are uncertain terms (2007:640).

Convention against torture and other cruel inhuman or degrading treatment or punishment

The Convention Against Torture and Other Cruel Inhuman or Degrading Treatment or Punishment[6] was accepted in 10.12.1984 by United Nations General Assembly (Farmer, 2008:21).

In accordance with the Article 3 paragraph 1.

"No State Party shall expel, return ("refouler") or extradite a person to another State where there are substantial grounds for believing that he would be in danger of being subjected to torture."

The Article 3 of the Convention does not have any exemption clause (Farmer, 2008:21) but provides a restricted protection because the principle *of non- refoulement* is conditioned to torture and the restricted definition of torture (Pirjola, 2007:648; Çiçekli, 2009:97; Uzun, 2012:37)[7].

---

[6] For the original text of the Convention see UN, Treaty Series, Vol.1465, p.113. http://www.ohchr.org/EN/ProfessionalInterest/Pages/CAT.aspx (last visited: 02.01.2014).

International covenant on civil and political rights

International Covenant on Civil and Political Rights was accepted by UN General Assembly decision dated 16 December and no. 2200A(XXI) and entered into force in 23 March 1976[8].

In accordance with article 6, *"Every human being has the inherent right to life. This right shall be protected by law. No one shall be arbitrarily deprived of his life In countries which have not abolished the death penalty, sentence of death may be imposed only for the most serious crimes in accordance with the law in force at the time of the commission of the crime and not contrary to the provisions of the present Covenant and to the Convention on the Prevention and Punishment of the Crime of Genocide. This penalty can only be carried out pursuant to a final judgement rendered by a competent court. When deprivation of life constitutes the crime of genocide, it is understood that nothing in this article shall authorize any State Party to the present Covenant to derogate in any way from any obligation assumed under the provisions of the Convention on the Prevention and Punishment of the Crime of Genocide. Anyone sentenced to death shall have the right to seek pardon or commutation of the sentence. Amnesty, pardon or commutation of the sentence of death may be granted in all cases. Sentence of death shall not be imposed for crimes committed by persons below eighteen years of age and shall not be carried out on pregnant women. Nothing in this article shall be invoked to delay or to prevent the abolition of capital punishment by any State Party to the present Covenant."*

In accordance with article 7, *"No one shall be subjected to torture or to cruel, inhuman or degrading treatment or punishment. In*

---

[7] In accordance with the Article 1, "the term "torture" means any act by which severe pain or suffering, whether physical or mental, is intentionally inflicted on a person for such purposes as obtaining from him or a third person information or a confession, punishing him for an act he or a third person has committed or is suspected of having committed, or intimidating or coercing him or a third person, or for any reason based on discrimination of any kind, when such pain or suffering is inflicted by or at the instigation of or with the consent or acquiescence of a public official or other person acting in an official capacity. It does not include pain or suffering arising only from, inherent in or incidental to lawful sanctions."

[8] For the original text of the Convenant see http://www.ohchr.org/en/professionalinterest/pages/ccpr.aspx (Last visited: 02.01.2014). Turkey is party to the Covenant. Official Gazette, 21.07.2003- No. 25175.

particular, no one shall be subjected without his free consent to medical or scientific experimentation."

In addition article 2 says, *"Each State Party to the present Covenant undertakes to respect and to ensure to all individuals within its territory and subject to its jurisdiction the rights recognized in the present Covenant, without distinction of any kind, such as race, colour, sex, language, religion, political or other opinion, national or social origin, property, birth or other status."*

These provisions in question are interpreted in the manner of involving the principle of *non –refoulement*[9] by the Human Rights Committee.

Geneva Convention relative to the protection of civilian persons in time of war

This Convention is the Fourth Convention of 1949 Geneva Conventions which are the fundamental texts of international humanitarian law[10]. In accordance with the Second Part of the Convention on Aliens in the territory of a party to the conflict, *"Protected persons shall not be transferred to a Power which is not a party to the Convention"* (article 45).

Final Act of the United Nations conference on the status of stateless persons

Article 4 of Final Act of the United Nations Conference on the Status of Stateless Persons[11] states that, "The Conference, "Being of the opinion that Article 33 of the Convention Relating to the Status of Refugees of 1951 is an expression of the generally accepted principle that no State should expel or return a person in any manner

---

[9] UN Human Rights Committe General Comment No.20, International Human Rights Instruments, UN Doc. HRI/GEN/I/Rev.7,10.03.1992, http://www.unhchr.ch/tbs/doc.nsf/(Symbol)/6924291970754969c12563ed004c8ae5 (Last visited: 23.11.2013).

[10] For the original text of the Convention see http://www.icrc.org/ihl/INTRO/380 (Last visited: 02.01.2014). Turkey is party to the Convention. Official Gazette, 30.01.1953- No. 8322.

[11] For the original text of the Final Act see UN, Treaty Series, Vol.360, p.117-24. https://treaties.un.org/doc/publication/UNTS/Volume%20360/v360.pdf (Last visited: 02.01.2014).

whatsoever to the frontiers of territories where his life or freedom would be threatened on account of his race, religion, nationality, membership of a particular social group or political opinion, "Has not found it necessary to include in the Convention Relating to the Status of Stateless Persons an article equivalent to Article 33 of the Convention Relating to the Status of Refugees of 1951."

Convention for the protection of human rights and fundamental freedoms

Several articles of Convention for the Protection of Human Rights and Fundamental Freedoms[12], provide protection for refugees and asylum seekers. The most significant of these articles are article 3, 8, 13 and 34 (Kabaalioglu & Eksi, 2004:507). To article 3 of Convention for the Protection of Human Rights and Fundamental Freedoms, *"No one shall be subjected to torture or to inhuman or degrading treatment or punishment."* This provision of the Convention was interpreted as involving the principle of *non – refoulement* by European Court of Human Rights[13].

In accordance with article 8, "Everyone has the right to respect for his private and family life, his home and his correspondence." Article 13 says that, "*Everyone whose rights and freedoms as set forth in this Convention are violated shall have an effective remedy before a national authority notwithstanding that the violation has been committed by persons acting in an official capacity.*" To article 34, "*The Court may receive applications from any person, non-governmental organisation or group of individuals claiming to be the victim of a violation by one of the High Contracting Parties of the*

[12] The original text of the Convention see http://conventions.coe.int/Treaty/en/Treaties/Html/005.htm (Last visited. 02.01.2014). Turkey is Party to the Convention. Official Gazette, 19.03.1954- No. 8662.

[13] Soering v. UK, Eur. Ct. H.R., Application No. 1403/88, Judgment of 07.07.1989; Chahal v. UK, Eur. Ct. H.R., Application No. 22414/93, Report of 27.06.1995; Ahmed. v. Austria, Eur. Ct. H.R., Application No. 25964, Judgement of 17.12.1996, Nsona v. Nedherlands 28.12.1996, Paez v. Sweden 30.10.1997, Othman (Abu Qatada) v. UK 17.01.2012, Jabarı v. Turkey, Eur. Ct. H.R., Application No. 40035/98, Judgement of 11.06.2000, Abdolkhani and Karimnia v. Turkey, Application Number 30471/08, ECHR-HUDOC, http://www.echr.coe.int/echr/en/hudoc (Last visited: 23.11.2013). For translation and consideration on case of Abdolkhani and Karimnia v. Turkey, see Ekşi (2010: 68 and 133); Ergüven & Özturhanlı (2013: 1041).

rights set forth in the Convention or the protocols thereto. The High Contracting Parties undertake not to hinder in any way the effective exercise of this right."

Turkish national law

The Law on Foreigners and International Protection (Law No. 6458) was adopted by the Turkish Grand National Assembly, 4 April 2013, published in Official Gazette 11 April 2013, upon approval of the president[14]. Law on Foreigners and International Protection has one direct and general provision and two indirect and specific provisions on the principle of *non refoulement.*

The General provision on the principle of *non-refoulement*

In accordance with the Article 4, "*No one who fall under the scope of this Law shall be returned to a place where he or she may be subject to torture, inhuman or degrading punishment or treatment, or where his or her life or freedom may be under threat on account of his or her race, religion, nationality, membership of a particular social group or political opinion.*"[15]

As a systematic interpretation, this provision is regulated in Chapter One that is entitled "*Purpose, Scope, Definitions and Non-refoulement*" and it is regulated in Section Two. This chapter

[14] Official Gazette, 11.04.2013- No. 28615. The original text of Law No. 6458 see http://www.resmigazete.gov.tr/eskiler/2013/04/20130411-2.htm (Last visited: 02.01.2014). For the unofficial translation of Law No. 6458 see http://www.refworld.org/docid/5167fbb20.html (Last visited: 02.01.2014). The Law came into force one year after the date of publication of the Law. (Article 125). Before Law on Foreigners and International Protection, foreigner's law was not regulated by general code. Also refugee protection in Turkey used to be regulated by secondary legislation. Regulation No. 1994/6169 on the Procedures and Principles related to Possible Population Movements and Aliens Arriving in Turkey either as Individuals or in Groups Wishing to Seek Asylum either from Turkey or Requesting Residence Permission in order to Seek Asylum From Another Country. The new Law repeals the provisions of the Law Related to Residence and Travel of Foreigners in Turkey (Law No.5683) entirely and the Passport Law (Law No. 5682) partially. Within this context new entry and residence regime has been established for foreigners and the new Law contains a comprehensive section on international protection. For the comparative list of the Law Related to Residence and Travel of Foreigners in Turkey, Passport Law and the new Law No.6458,

[15] For translation see http://www.refworld.org/docid/5167fbb20.html (Last visited: 02.01.2014).

includes purposes, scope and definitions and *non – refoulement* for all foreigners. In this context, the principle of *non-refoulement* has been recognised for all foreigners including refugees, asylum seekers, foreigners who entered into Turkey legally or illegally or foreigners who have not entered into Turkey yet (Ergüven & Özturhanlı, 2013: 1040; also see Ekşi, 2008: 2832; Taneri, 2012: 241).

Secondly, as a substantial consideration, the article four includes almost all conditions for *non – refoulement* that have been mentioned by international conventions. Thirdly, on the contrary to the 1951 Convention, the general provision on the principle of *non-refoulement* does not regulate any exception clause.

Draft version of Law on Foreigners and International Protection had an exception clause by reference to 1951 Convention. In the report of Turkish Grand National Assembly of Turkey Human Rights Investigation Commission[16], article four, paragraph one was interpreted as in harmony with international law and related jurisprudence, preventive for proceedings that would patently result against Turkey. However the report emphasized that there was a requirement for application of the principle of *non-refoulement* without exception. It is stated in the report that the principle of *non-refoulement* is one of the fundamental principles of international human rights law and refugee law and it is a part of international customary law[17]. This nuance is relatively crucial for practice. In this context a refugee who constitutes a danger to the community of the country may be repatriated under 1951 Convention but shall not be repatriated under Turkish national law[18].

Specific provisions on the principle of *non-refoulment*

a. The Foreigners against whom a deportation decision shall not be issued.

In Section Four, under the title of "deportation", article 54 regulates the conditions of deportation[19]. Article 55 settles the

---

[16] For full text of the report of Turkish Grand National Assembly of Turkey Human Rights Investigation Commission see http://www.tbmm.gov.tr/sirasayi/donem24/yil01/ss310.pdf (Last visited: 03.02.2014)

[17] The report of Turkish Grand National Assembly of Turkey Human Rights Investigation Commission, p.16.

[18] For the counter-view see, Ergüven & Özturhanlı (2013: 1044).

foreigners against whom a deportation decision shall not be issued regardless of whether they fall under the scope of article 54.

In accordance with the article 55/1-a, "*Regardless of whether they fall under the scope of Article 54 of this Law, a deportation decision shall not be issued against those: for whom there are serious indications that he or she will be subjected to the death penalty, torture, cruel or degrading treatment or punishment in the country to which they will be deported,...*"[20].

Dardağan-Kibar finds that this provision is a manifestation of the principle of n*on-refoulement* and it is in harmony with article 4 (2012:62). Bayraktaroğlu-Özçelik states that Article 55/1-a is in harmony with case law of the European Court of Human Rights concerning Article 3 of Convention for the Protection of Human Rights and Fundamental Freedoms (2013:233). Moreover, the terms of "serious indications" are more protective than the terms of "subject to" within article 4 (Bayraktaroğlu-Özçelik, 2013:235).

---

[19] Article 54: (1) A deportation decision may be issued against foreigners: a) For whom a deportation decision is deemed necessary pursuant to Article 59 of the Law No. 5237, b) Who are a leader, member, supporter or of a terrorist or a benefit-oriented criminal organization, c) Who use false information and fraudulent documents in procedures concerning entry into Turkey, visa and residence permits, ç) Who make a living through illegitimate means during their stay in Turkey, d) Who constitute a threat to public order and security or public health, e) Who exceed the duration of visa or visa exemption more than 10 days, or those whose visa has been cancelled, f) Whose residence permits are cancelled g) Who hold residence permits but exceed the duration of the residence permit for more than 10 days without an acceptable excuse, ğ) Who are identified as having been working without a work permit, h) Who violate the provisions on legal entry into or legal exit from Turkey, ı) Who are identified as having arrived in Turkey despite a valid ban on entry, i) From among persons whose applications for international protection are rejected, who are excluded from international protection, whose applications are considered as inadmissible, who withdraw their application, whose applications are deemed to be withdrawn, whose international protection statuses have ceased or have been cancelled, those who are not entitled to stay in Turkey pursuant to any other provision of this Law following a final decision, j) From among persons whose applications for the extension of residence permits have been rejected, those who do not leave Turkey within 10 days.

(2) Among applicants or beneficiaries of international protection, a deportation decision may be issued only when there are serious indications to believe that such persons constitute a threat to the security of the State, or when such persons are convicted of a crime which constitutes a threat to public order. For the conditions of deportation see, Bayraktaroğlu-Özçelik (2013: 218-232).

[20] For translation see http://www.refworld.org/docid/5167fbb20.html (Last visited: 02.01.2014).

b. Subsidiary Protection

Under the title of "Subsidiary Protection", article 63 regulates a derivative concept of complementary protection in international refugee law.

In accordance with article 63, "A foreigner or a stateless person who could neither be qualified as a refugee nor a conditional refugee, yet who is unable or, due to the threat concerned, is unwilling to avail himself or herself of the protection of his or her country of origin or the country of habitual residence, shall be granted subsidiary protection status following the status determination procedures if he or she will face;

a) the death penalty or execution,

b) torture or inhuman or degrading treatment or punishment,

c) serious threat to his or her person by reason of indiscriminate violence in situations of international or internal armed conflict, upon return to his or her country of origin or country of habitual residence[21]

.

Thus it is clearly seen that the principle of *non-refoulement* is accepted not only for refugees or asylum seekers but also for all foreigners by Turkish Foreigners Law (Ergüven & Özturhanlı, 2013: 1035).

Conclusion

As a conclusion, it is obvious that in Turkish national law, the principle of *non-refoulement* is regulated with quite comprehensive nature. Unlike the Convention Relating to the Status of Refugees, New Law on Foreigners and International Protection regulates the principle of *non-refoulement* for all foreigners without any exemption clause. The conditions for the principle of *non-refoulement* are wider than the Convention Against Torture and Other Cruel Inhuman or Degrading Treatment or Punishment. Also new Law on Foreigners and International Protection has both directly and indirectly provisions on principle of *non-refoulement* which are different from International Covenant on Civil and Political Rights and Convention

[21] For translation see http://www.refworld.org/docid/5167fbb20.html (Last visited: 02.01.2014).

for the Protection of Human Rights and Fundamental Freedoms. Moreover Turkish national law is in harmony with case law of European Court of Human Rights.

Chapter 4: To What Extent Are Migrant Workers' Rights Positioned within the Discourse of Human Rights?

Süreyya Sönmez Efe

"World community has entered into the varying degrees in to a universal community and violation of rights in one part of the world is felt everywhere...the idea of cosmopolitan right is therefore not fantastic and overstrained; it is a necessary complement to the unwritten code of political and international rights, transforming it into a universal right of humanity. Only under this condition can we flatter ourselves that we are continually advancing towards perpetual peace" (Immanuel Kant, 1795).

This statement succinctly summarises an ideal picture of an international system of rights through the lenses of cosmopolitanism; the only way to accomplish perpetual peace is to have a universal system of rights that makes states and people responsible for their actions and holds them to account within a realm of universal responsibility i.e. ICC (International Criminal Court) is an example of a cosmopolitan approach to moral and legal conduct of states/individuals. The cosmopolitan approach helps us to establish a universal system of law on the grounds of moral values. Thus, in this paper, I aim to analyse the rights of migrant workers taking a Human Rights (HR) based approach in the light of the concept of cosmopolitanism. I will explore the key components of cosmopolitan right which are as follows in this context; migrant workers as autonomous agents, the state and universal system of rights (UN agencies). I will then look at the key factors that become an obstacle for recognition of migrant workers' rights.

First I will analyse the state sovereignty. State sovereignty poses either as a challenge to the universal system of law that lays out the rights of migrant workers; or according to Kant's concept of cosmopolitanism, it becomes the core element of the system of rights by acting as a moral agent-the morality of the states are reinforced by subscription to universal moral/legal rights i.e. signing up to the UN HR Conventions.

I will then look at the conversation of the legal rights of migrant workers at International HR Organisations and the states' attitudes towards the core Universal HR Conventions concerning the rights of migrant workers. Within this section, I will explore the definition of 'migrant worker' and the key reasons for nation states' lack of interest into these conventions.

Thirdly, I will look at the 2008 Global Economic Crisis (GEC) which is the second factor that affects the recognition and implementation of HR conventions concerning migrant workers by nation states. I will analyse the impact of the 2008 GEC on global migration flows in general and on migrant workers in particular.

Fourthly, national immigration policies is my final analysis in this paper to show the impact of the GEC on the rights of migrant workers and the role of state sovereignty in implementation of the HR conventions concerning the rights of migrant workers within their territories. I will closely look at the impact of the GEC on the Turkish economy and immigration policy. The analysis of Turkish immigration policy will allow me to draw conclusions to see whether protection of migrant workers is the priority of the nation states' policies or not.

The Concept of A 'Human Rights-based Approach' to Migrant Workers' Rights

In this section I will look at the Migrant Workers' Rights (MWR) through the lenses of cosmopolitanism and its core principles in order to analyse a 'Human Rights based approach' to MWR. A cosmopolitan approach allows us to incorporate two mainstream fields of HR discourse; moral right and legal right. The concept of cosmopolitanism recognises the interconnectedness of the peoples from different states in the world and lays out its principles on the grounds of intrinsic value and common humanity; which are also among the fundamental principles of core HR Conventions. Many UN agencies, international and national organisations recognize migrant rights as human rights which are universal, inalienable and indivisible; and they must be protected everywhere (Ruhs, 2013, p.2).

Moral philosophical arguments of 'right' allow us to conceptualise the moral standing of MWR at international and national levels. One of the fundamental principles of HR is to realise and guarantee human dignity which is defined as 'intrinsic worth' that is, an unconditional worth that every human enjoys by virtue of humanity (Gewirth, 1992, in Minkler, 2013, p.6). The principle of 'worthiness of individual' is an essential element of Kant's concept of cosmopolitan right (CR). David Held (2010, p.230) explains cosmopolitan values through a set of principles which can be universally shared in order to protect and nurture every individual's *"equal significance in the moral realm of humanity"*. He focuses on eight core principles which are as follows; *"(1) equal worth and dignity; (2) active agency; (3) personal responsibility and accountability; (4) consent; (5) collective decision making about public matters through voting procedures; (6) inclusiveness and subsidiarity; (7) avoidance of serious harm; and (8) sustainability"* (ibid). Thus, these principles value every person equally; consider them as autonomous agents for their actions; free as they can vote and have political participation; and he/she does not harm any other human being.

When we talk about the legal right, there is a 'right' holder who enjoys the rights and freedoms; and there is a duty bearer who has responsibility to grant these rights and freedoms. Here, I consider 'migrant workers' as right holders and nation-states (and their immigration policies) as duty bearers. In this context, in order for the right holder (migrant worker) to enjoy the fundamental rights, he/she must act based on his/her autonomy by using agency. In order to accomplish human autonomy and agency, right holder's certain needs must be fulfilled, which provides a rationale for certain HR principles, such as an adequate standard of living (Copp, 1992). Moreover, in order to enjoy human agency, the right holder needs to have certain freedoms assured in the HR catalogue. The moral obligation of the duty holder (here I refer to states) is to recognize the fundamental freedoms and needs of persons (migrant workers) in order for them to act as autonomous agents. In other words, for migrant workers to act as autonomous agents and enjoy fundamental freedoms depends on how these rights are granted by the states as duty holders. In order for the states to implement the international HR law concerning MWR in their national jurisdiction, there needs to be a universal legal system that provides guidelines/ benchmarks regarding the fundamental rights and freedoms of migrant works and allow them to exercise their rights as they see fit.

The legal right on moral grounds is addressed in Immanuel Kant's concept of cosmopolitanism that is based on the principle of common humanity, which encompasses the following freedoms; every person's freedom of will and his/her freedom of movement and travel to go beyond one's limit of outer freedom and ethnocentric boundaries. CR essentially, gives individuals the right to seek to communicate with other individuals from other lands and cultures (Kant, [1795] (1923) p.444). The motives of these contacts may vary; it can be cultural, economic or commercial and religious interactions. Thus, according to this principle of CR persons can pursue better jobs with better economic conditions and living standards in another country and can become an economic migrant and co-exist within the host community without causing harm. In other words, migrant workers can work in the countries other than their own, however, the foreigner/stranger's purpose of visit cannot go beyond a "*peaceful pursuit of their meant of livelihood upon the territory of another*" (Benhabib, 2004, p.38).

This principle of legal rights based on moral values exists in many UN agencies and NGOs concerning migrant workers that responded to states' national immigration restrictions by emphasising the MWR as being HR (Ruhs, 2013, p.2). These rights are inalienable (they cannot be denied to any human being, and should not be transferable and saleable), indivisible (political and civil rights cannot be separated from social and cultural rights) and universal (they apply everywhere) which derive from a common humanity (ibid).

Second and First Generation Rights Dichotomy

However, the argument of a first and second generation rights dichotomy within universal covenants can be considered as an obstacle in the definition and recognition of MWR universally.

There is an inherent hierarchy of rights made within two universal HR conventions; the UN Convention on Economic, social and cultural rights (ESCR) and the UN Convention on civil and political rights (ICPR).

First generation rights conceptualise HR within the framework of "*negative rights*", freedoms from; for example the articles 2-21 on Universal Declaration of Human Rights are categorised as first generation rights (freedom from slavery and involuntary servitude is one of them). The first generation rights also favours laissez faire type of economics based on free and competitive trade with a maximum individual choice and a minimum state regulation and intervention. In other words, in negative rights, the abstention is favoured over intervention of government in the quest of human dignity (Claude and Weston, 2006, p.21).

Second generation rights, on the other hand, emphasise the malpractices of individual liberty within capitalist development, which criticises the exploitation of the working class. These rights are classed as positive rights with the terms 'rights to' used in principle. These types of rights favour functioning state welfare with maximum state/government intervention in order to safeguard and assure equitable production and distribution of values and/or capabilities. In this context, Economic, Social and Cultural Rights have three main categories; rights to an adequate standard of living, adequate food and nutrition rights, clothing, housing, and the necessary conditions of care. Importantly, second generation rights focus on social equality and are influenced by the concepts of socialism, communism and the emergence of the third world and its influence on international affairs.

First generation rights proponents exclude second and also third generation (solidarity rights) rights altogether and label them as derivative. The danger of the exclusion of second and third generation rights is that they can be considered 'grey areas' and be overlooked, including legal status of the migrant workers. These grey areas fundamentally stem from the status of migrant workers, which becomes interchangeable as a result of free movement of migrant workers based on capitalism, globalisation and the free market. There are some articles in the Universal Declaration of Human Rights which are interconnected and therefore, inseparable from first, second or even third generation rights; for example, 'the right to free choice of employment and join trade unions' fundamentally comes under second and third generation rights which is categorised as collective rights (second) and economic/social self-determination (third). However, if a migrant worker becomes a victim of human trafficking as a result of denial of 'free choice of employment', he/she will be a victim of slavery which is safeguarded by the first generation rights.

The problem is the relationship between the 'right holder' and the 'duty bearer' mentioned above gets murkier when the distinction is made between negative and positive rights. Although there is minimum/or no state intervention on negative rights, I believe states are responsible for recognition and implementation of both negative and positive rights. Kant's concept of CR does not make this distinction as according to cosmopolitanism individuals and states are equally responsible for their actions as they are considered as moral agents. As a result, acting as moral agents, states have responsibility to protect individuals' rights. At this point, the relationship between state sovereignty and universal law needs to be analysed in order to answer the following question; would nation states compromise their sovereignty to universal law and take a HR approach to MW's rights?

The question of sovereignty

There are three contemporary definitions of sovereignty; 'Westphalian Sovereignty', 'Liberal International Sovereignty' (Held, 2002, pp.45-7, Krasner, 1999, p.20-25) and 'Cosmopolitan Sovereignty' (Held, 2002, p.45). Westphalian sovereignty is defined as free and equal states that enjoy ultimate authority over its subjects and objects. States' relationships with other sovereigns are voluntary and contingent that leaves room to transitory military and economic alliances, cultural and religious affinities (Benhabib, 2004, p.40). In this model, "*States regard cross-border processes as a 'private matter' concerning only those immediately affected*" (Held, 2002, p.4).

In liberal international sovereignty, states' equality highly depends on their observance of common values and principles, such as; HR, Rule of Law and respect for democratic self-determination. Thus, state is not an ultimate authority and it is obliged to treat its citizens according to certain norms where individuals can have freedom of choice to participate in free market, freedom of speech and association.

In cosmopolitan sovereignty' (ibid), international law is considered as a system of public law, which properly limits not just political power but all forms of social power. Thus, cosmopolitan sovereignty locates the dominance of individual human beings as moral and political agents and accountability of power-law of peoples (Rawls, 1999). Kant emphasises on the principle of morality in universal law and person's capacity of reason and freedom as key elements to achieve the universal law. Kant attributes moral personality to states on the grounds of the ownership of free will, therefore, states and persons become the same kinds of beings with the possession of will which makes them the same type of moral agents (Flikschuh, 2010, p.480). This analogy shows that the relationship between the states and persons ought to be equal on the grounds of the principle of morality. However, when we look at the states and the individuals from juridical terms, they are not similar on the grounds of possession of sovereignty and the coercion of a superior authority will take away their distinctive moral personality.

All three models, however, place the 'state' at the core of the legal or moral structure and its sovereignty is either an obstacle against the ideal of global political and social justice or it is something to be negotiated. The international HR treaties are established for the protection of individual human beings; however the obligations that come from these treaties are for states (Donnelly, 1999, p.85). For example, the universal covenants of HR oblige states to implement these norms on their own citizens, in other words, internationally recognised rights apply only to the residents. However, the foreigners living in a foreign land are subject to state jurisdiction and control/ regulation of the host country whose citizens enjoy the universal rights.

I argue that although states play in a key role in universal system of rights, CR and sovereignty act complementary as two non-opposite poles. When the states act as moral agents, as the duty holders of fundamental rights, sovereignty can be used to implement the universal law- e.g. implementation of the Convention on Migrant Workers at national level. As a result, sovereignty becomes something that can be negotiable and transformed which can be used as a tool to reframe RMW at national level. The following section focuses on the conventions on migrant workers' rights at international law which will show the states attitudes towards protection of RMW.

Human rights of migrants at international arena

ILO (1919) is the first organisation (later became UN special agency) that emphasised the 'protection of interests of workers when employed in countries other than their own" (ILO, 2012) referring to the migrant workers (MW). There are two ILO conventions that particularly focus on the rights of MW; Migration for Employment Convention NO.97 (1949) and the Convention on Migrant Workers (Supplementary Provisions) NO. 143.

The convention No. 97 essentially plays an instrumental role in regulating of international migration. The Convention No.97 does not define MW and their rights explicitly. Convention No.143 starts with strong and promising statements in identifying RMW where it states *"protecting the interest of workers when employed in countries other than their own' and 'labour is not a commodity'"* (ILO, 1975). This statement clearly defines MW outside of 'market terms' and locate them into the HR language; which takes a big step by pointing out that MW cannot be exploited as a result of market failures. However, both ILO conventions fall short with not being comprehensive enough in terms of setting out clear fundamental rights for MW.

There was clearly a need for an international convention, which deals specifically with the issues of MW. The drafting process of the United Nation International Convention on the Protection of the Rights of all Migrant Workers and their families (ICRMW) started in 1980 and it was in 1990 (came into force in 2003) when it was drafted. This Convention is different from its predecessors for the following reasons; first, the ICRMW has the most comprehensive definition of MW than any other international organization; second, it explicitly lays out what types of rights that MW should have; third, the differentiation between negative and positive right abovementioned is not made in this convention. This convention urges the states to establish minimum standards for MW regardless of their legal status; which applies to regular as well as irregular/informal migrants and requires states to protect them from exploitation. Nevertheless, stateless persons have been excluded from this definition, which can make it difficult to deal with individual cases in terms of migrant workers who may be subjects of human trafficking and exploitation.

The low number of ratifications of the ICRMW by nation-states shows lack of interest in the universalised law regarding MW's rights. The ICRMW is ratified by few countries which are predominantly migrant sending countries rather than migrant receiving countries. There are three main reasons for this; one is the lengthy drafting process of the convention and the frequent changes of members of the UN Committee in charge of drafting the convention has weakened the importance of the language of HR within the context of MW. Second, the nation-states are concerned that the ICRMW includes the protection of irregular migrants, which will be costly to their welfare system. Third, the nation-states are determined to keep their sovereignty intact by adopting their own immigration policies and making their own decisions on RMW; therefore, a universal law that restrict the states' ability of decision making on their immigration policies would not be desirable. The problem is the possible clash of countries' national law with international law concerning MW's rights. For example, some countries, such as Germany, claim that their national policies already address these rights and are compatible with the UN Convention (Ruhs, 2013, p.18-19).

In addition to the key factors for the major migrant receiving countries lack of interest in the ICRMW, the cost and benefit of protecting migrant workers during economic downturns becomes a major issue for the states. Thus, the next section will briefly look at the impact of 2008 Economic Crisis on the rights of migrant workers.

Global economic crisis and its impact on migrant workers

This section will look at three main points; one, the impact of 2008 Global Economic Crisis (GEC) on the global market and sectors; two, economic and social implications of the GEC on migrant workers; three, the nation-states' immigration policies' response to the GEC.

The 2008 GEC is different from recessions happened in the 1970s and 1990s because it did not started in developing countries; it started in the USA and spread to other industrial countries (e.g. the

UK) and then other developing countries (Martin, 2009, p.673). The countries that are affected by the GEC are the most are predominantly migrant receiving countries. The sectors that have been attracting MW are mainly affected by the crisis such as; agriculture, construction, manufacturing, service and hospitality. For example, the US construction sector, in which two-thirds of the workers are MW, was hit by the crisis severely and the unemployment rate rose sharply; from 7.5 to 13.2 million between 2007 and 2009 (Martin, 2009, 676). The Economic Crisis affected the migrant sending countries too, such as Bangladesh; whose economy highly depended on the remittances.

MW is particularly vulnerable during economic downturns because the economic crisis places them in a precarious status in the global market. After the GEC, the labour market witnessed shrinking employment opportunities, which mainly affected the sectors (e.g. construction) where migrant workers were predominantly recruited (the ILO, 2009, p.30). According to the ILO report (ibid), persons of foreign origin and migrants are hit by job losses the most because they are laid off disproportionately. Moreover, migrant workers have become the victims of worsening economic conditions with less pay, insecurity and reduction in working time. The low-skilled and poor migrant workers are worse off in times of economic crisis because they have limited chance of mobility in the global market; as a result these migrants are pushed to work in the informal economy working with an irregular status and are deprived from having access to safety nets and support mechanisms, which further reduced during the GEC (McCabe and Meissner, 2010, p.7). Undocumented workers are not entitled to welfare benefits or social protection and consequently suffer the hardships more acutely during the recession (Papademetreou et al, 2009 in Philips, p.262). Furthermore, migrant workers are pushed to adapt themselves to changes in the labour market therefore; they end up accepting jobs with more abusive and substandard conditions than before (ibid).

There are also social implications of the GEC on the migrant workers. Migrant workers are scapegoated for loss of job opportunities and witnessed xenophobic and discriminatory violence which is on the rise in the world. According to the ILO, there is a rise in far right political movements, increased murders and lynchings of migrants in some countries and an existence of anti-immigrant sentiment and hostile political discourse against the foreigners (ibid). However, the statistical evidence shows that immigrants are hit hardest by the crisis in terms of job losses. Unemployment of immigrants in OECD countries increased after the economic crisis as a result of rising involuntary part-time work and decreasing temporary employment; for example, in countries, such as, Belgium, United Kingdom, Norway, Spain, and so on, 50% or more of the labour-force working in temporary employment consist of immigrants, hence, the short term impact of recession on immigrants is rather alarming (OECD, 2009). Thus, during economic crisis MW are more exposed to job losses that occur in global and regional markets.

The impact of the GEC on remittances also an important point to show the effect of the economic crisis on the migrant sending countries and the returnee migrant workers. According to the ILO, migrant remittances to countries of origin are declining (ibid) and there are fewer opportunities for the returnees in the countries of origins (ibid). Thus, because many origin countries are hit by the crises and had scarce job opportunities, most migrant workers prefer to stay put in the destination countries and most probably work in worse conditions. Castles and Miller (2010, p.4) also point out the reason why migrant workers do not repatriate and prefer to stay in destination countries is because the economic conditions are worse in their own countries. This shows that unlike the early predictions, there has not been a significant decrease in migration stock because migrant workers are most severely affected by unemployment and economic/social hardships during recessions.

The third concern of the impact of GEC on MW is the tightened immigration policies of the migrant receiving countries. The nation-states introduce new deliberate policies promoting exclusion and expulsion of migrant workers, or altering existing policies with reducing quotas or intake of foreign workers (the ILO, 2009, p.30). Some of the examples of the countries that introduced restrictive immigration policies for migrant workers are as follows; the UK has tightened its 'Point Based System' with increasing wage and skills thresholds (Green and Winters, 2010, p.23); Australia has cut its skilled permanent migrant quota for 2009 by 20% (ibid). Spain has cut its quota for non-seasonal 'Contingente' workers from 15,000

(2008) to 900 (2009) (OECD, 2009a in ibid); Italy cut its quota for non-seasonal MW from 150,000 in 2008 to zero in 2009 (ibid); Return Programmes have been introduced in countries, such as, Japan, Spain and Czech Republic, which offered compensation to unemployed immigrants to leave the country (Tilly, 2011, p.686). An alternative restriction to cut immigration flow is limiting the number of work-permits introduced by the following countries in 2009; Russia, USA, Australia and Kazakhstan (Abella and Ducanes, 2009; Fix et al, 2009; Graglia, 2009; Martin, 2009). Malaysia and Singapore implemented harsher policies by publicly urging the employers to lay off immigrants before native workers (Abella and Ducanes, 2009; Green and Winters, 2010). Denmark has begun to check passports of entrants from the EU countries by which it has broken with EU protocol.

The next section will look at how Turkey is affected by the GEC; how Turkish immigration policy has been shaped as a result of this; and whether it has a rights based approach to migrant workers or not.

The Case of Turkey

Recovery of Turkish economy from the crisis

Turkey has not been affected by the 2008 Economic crisis in the same way as Europe and the USA, on the contrary, it was one of the emerging markets with a high grow rate (Tetik, 2012, p.39). It was the banking sector that made the 2008 Economic crisis spread; however, because of the measures that Turkey had taken after the 2001 crisis, the banking sector was not affected as such by the GEC (Karagöz, 2009). Turkey has become the fastest growing country in Europe with 8.9% in 2010 while the world in general has been trying to recover from the crisis (Tetik, 2012, p.42). Turkey's foreign policy and its new diplomatic dialogue with Middle-East and Africa is an important point to address here which is highly related to its promotion of Foreign Direct Investment (FDI) and migration policy; for example, the country opted for relaxed visa requirements with the countries that have trade agreements; such as Africa, Middle East, Latin America and Eastern European Countries including Russia. The positive outcome of this promotion is felt in the tourism sector, health tourism, number of overseas students and the construction sector.

Unemployment is also falling which was 9.8 per cent in 2011, down from 11.9 per cent in 2010; unemployment fell further to 8.9 per cent in 2012.

However, the informal economy in Turkey needs to be emphasised here in terms of underlining the issues of labour rights and standards of unreported workers. According to the EU Progress Report (2012, p.66), "*Turkey has adopted a second Action Plan to Fight the Informal Economy (2011–2013). The ratio of undeclared workers to the total of all employed as measured by the Turkish Statistical Institute decreased by 3.3 per cent, but it is still close to 40 per cent...*" As mentioned above, informal economy is one of the key culprits for exploitation of migrant workers; as migrant workers work in precarious conditions with minimum or no protection and social security.

Turkey's immigration policy

Turkey is not a 'new' country of immigration; historically there have been significant inflows of migrants, particularly from the Balkans (throughout 20th century). Because there has been a large influx of immigration into Europe in the 1960s, Turkey has been characterised as a country of emigration on the international migration scene (Kirişçi, 2007). "*While Turkey remains a "sending country," with a net population outflow of 50,000 in 2010, emigration numbers have significantly decreased since their peak of 370,000 (net) in 1980*" (Best, 2013, p.3). According to the World Bank, Turkey has become a destination country for migrants in 2012 (The World Bank, 2014). The question that I am seeking to explore in this section is; is Turkish immigration policy ready for this change? And how far is a 'rights based approach' to migrant workers taken by Turkish immigration policy in the current economic climate?

Turkey's immigration policy had been one dimensional and based on nationalism until the last decade; it was based on the Law on Settlement of 1934, which mainly covered the immigrants of Turkish origin or culture; and their rights were addressed after the settlement in the country (Kirişçi, 1996, p.93). However, the language of rights concerning foreigners is not new for Turkey. Turkey was among the drafters and first signatories of the Geneva Convention (1951), which created Turkey's Asylum Policy (Frelick, 1997). Moreover, Turkey has ratified the ICRMW in 2004 which is an important step forward in terms of recognition of the rights of regular migrant workers as well as irregular migrants.

Secondly, as part of the accession process to the EU, Turkey has adopted the immigration law that complies with the EU Law on immigration. Turkey has started a number of reforms within its legal system starting from 2002. These reforms impacted the domain of asylum and migration too. For example, as a part of the first reform package, the Law on Work Permits for Foreign Nationals was adopted in 2003, the Law on Citizenship was amended and the additional protocols against migrant smuggling and human trafficking of the United Nations Convention against Transnational Organized Crime were adopted. The other issue was visa policy and border management that is included in the harmonisation package during this period (ibid). However, although Turkey adopted the negative list of the Schengen agreement in this period; after 2005, Turkey began to change its visa regulations based on new political agreements with new countries; for example, in 2009, Turkey agreed to lift visa requirements with Albania, Jordan and Libya; in 2010 with Russia, Serbia and Lebanon; and in 2011 with Bahrain, Malaysia, Qatar and Kyrgyzstan (ibid).

Although there have been many reforms concerning migrants, most notably the Law on Foreigners and International Protection in 2013; the original intent of the 1934 law remains evident in both legislation and practice (Best, 2013, p.2). The positive effects of the New Law on Foreigners are yet to be seen. In order to remain loyal to the negotiations with the EU accession, the Turkish government has evidently rejected large-scale reforms to the immigration system, instead favouring more limited measures (ibid). After the GEC, many EU countries opted for more restricted immigration policies for migrant workers; which in turn affected Turkey's immigration policy. In other words, currently, Turkey follows the EU approach to immigration which is based on regulating migration, protectionism of the borders and immigration control rather than rights based policies.

Thus, the recent economic developments, the EU accession process, Turkish new foreign policy and Turkish nationalism become important in designing Turkish immigration policy. All these factors usually place the state interests and the interests of Turkish citizens before the interests and the rights of migrant workers. Although Turkey recognized MWR by ratifying the ICRMW, the key factors that affect and shape Turkish immigration policy show that there is still problem of having a rights based approach to issues of migrant workers. This example also shows that states can opt to become a part of universal system of rights, however, this is a voluntary position and there are other factors affect the states' actions in real world.

Conclusion

This paper asked whether it is possible to opt for a HR approach to RMW. First of all, I have analysed RMW from the perspective of cosmopolitan rights, and looked at the international conventions which address the legal rights and status of MW. The paper looked at two main factors for the main migrant receiving countries reluctance of ratifying the ICRMW; state sovereignty and economic interests particularly during the economic downturns. The concept of sovereignty is analysed in order to show the role of the states in protecting and promoting rights of migrant workers within their territories. This analysis shows that states are willing to keep their ability to make full decisions on their immigration policies without an intervention by the International Law. This can be considered as one of the most important reasons of the major migrant receiving countries for not signing the ICRMW.

Secondly, the paper looked at the impact of the 2008 economic crisis on migrant workers and concluded that migrant workers are affected negatively who have become more vulnerable to job losses and exploitation. In the times of crisis, states opt for more restrictive immigration policies in order to aid a rapid economic recovery. This is evident from the examples from the immigration policies from both developed and developing countries abovementioned which are not migrant friendly.

The last section of the paper focused on Turkish immigration policy after the economic crisis in order to answer the question 'to what extent are migrant workers' rights positioned within a discourse of HR?' First, this section looked at reaction of the Turkish economy to the 2008 GEC briefly. Second, the key factors that shape Turkish immigration policy are mentioned which are; Turkey's foreign policy, the EU immigration policy, the 2008 GEC and the current reforms in Turkish immigration policy. Turkish current foreign policy and trade agreements with the countries outside of the EU single market have influenced its strategies of immigration policy and visa requirements.

All in all, this analysis show that migrant workers are not fully treated from HR perspective in most countries as the national and economic interests are paramount over the interests of migrant workers. The main factors for this is as follows; first, the status of the MW is predominantly determined within the countries' national policies and the tightened immigration policies after the GEC shows that it is unlikely for MW to have more rights in host countries; such as, access to legal protection in case of abuse by the employer. Second, although Turkey ratified the ICRMW, the issue of irregular MW still needs to be addressed legally. Third, Turkey's accession process to the EU may pose a hurdle for Turkish immigration policy to implement MW's rights in line with ICRMW as none of the EU countries have ratified the Convention; and the immigration policies of the many EU countries are restrictive.

Thus, we are still far from having cosmopolitan ideals of right where RMW are still primarily decided by the nation-states' immigration policies which do not have a right-based-approach to immigration. However, it is crucial to have a UN Convention that defines MW in an international domain and spreads the language of rights globally; as a result the rights that are established in this treaty will set a benchmark for nation states to recognize the basic rights of migrant workers and include them in their immigration policies.

Chapter 5: In the Nexus of Stigma or Prestige: Politicians with Migration-background

Devrimsel Deniz Nergiz

The political participation of Mowassat, Özkan, or Sharma alongside Schmidt, Maier, or Beck is already a routine part of German politics. But scholar interest has not yet been directed towards politicians with migration backgrounds in Germany. Politicians, as the faces of political parties, are not only the movers of electoral politics. Diversity among party faces hints at the composition of the given society and its politics.

In spring 2008, when this research took off, North Rhine-Westphalia, Baden-Württemberg and Bavaria, states with the biggest migrant populations, had no politicians with migration background in their state parliaments. This changed as of the 2010, 2011 and 2013 elections, respectively. In the federal parliament, on the other hand, the 16th legislative period hosted 11 politicians with migration backgrounds, while the 17th legislative period, which convened in September 2009, hosted 20. Furthermore, during the last two years, three ministers and two state secretaries with migration backgrounds have been appointed in Lower Saxony, Baden-Württemberg and North Rhine-Westphalia, respectively. During the period of study, one politician with migration background has become the co-chair of his party while another politician in another political party has been named vice-chair.

The interest in politicians with particularly Turkey origin can probably be best illustrated by Berlin state legislature elections in autumn 2009, when six candidates of Turkey origin from different political parties competed in the district of Kreuzberg. It has never before been the case that all mainstream political parties, in addition to novice parties such as the Pirate Party and BIG, had nominated candidates with migration backgrounds, specifically with Turkey origin, for the same electoral district. Also in the federal elections 2013, a growing interest towards politicians with migration background was observable: For the first time in the political history, a Turkish origin Muslim woman and an Afro-German man have been elected to represent the Christian Democratic Union at federal level. Overall the number of MPs with migration background increased up to 37 from 22.

Accompanying the demographic change in Germany, these examples seem to hint at the beginning of an era hallmarked by transformation of the composition of political representatives as well. It obviously underlines that almost all German political parties have become quite well-accustomed to recognize and recruit people with migration backgrounds, not only in the electoral lists but also in promising positions in their structures.

The question of who politicians with migration backgrounds represent, how they do so, and of why and where they act politically is not only an academic issue to be scrutinised by normative and empirical sources, but is at the same time an issue of current public interest. To give but one example, when Aygül Özkan was nominated to the ministry at the state level, as the first politician of Muslim faith, media reports placed great emphasis on what they saw as the contradiction between her religion and her party membership with the Christian Democrats. They also discussed the oath she had to take; her cultural origins from Turkey were also frequently mentioned. This exemplifies three preoccupations common in public discourse on politicians with immigration backgrounds: their party preferences, their religious affiliations, and their or their parents' countries of origin.

To that end, this article points to a lack of knowledge concerning how markers of difference or of diversity may be negotiated and deployed during the careers of politicians with migration backgrounds. To put it succinctly, this study examines using sociological tools of inquiry what it means—in political practice and career—for a politician to have an immigration background. In this manner the findings of this research reversed earlier approaches to the question "*what difference markers make in politics*" (Swain, 1993; Phillips, 1995), asking instead how the marker can be deployed in order not to make a difference. This makes the study unique, as it departs from the mainstream of this fledgling cottage industry by placing the experience and interpretation of political processes by the parliamentarians themselves at the centre of the research. This is important because it helps to connect the issues to broader concerns in the social sciences, namely to normality and exoticism, and to heterogeneities and inequalities (Wortham and Rhodes, 2013; Faist, 2013; Rosello, 2001; Kastoryano, 2002).

Political representation by diversity groups is more than the sum of mandates

Representative tasks in politics by diversity groups have always been a matter of scholarly interest (Bird, 2005; Kymlicka and Norman, 2000; Verba et. al., 1995) In the mainstream literature the discussion of representation took two paths: one of them is the process of recruitment, as mentioned above, while another perspective extends beyond the nomination and recruitment processes and concentrates on the substantial political goods to be gained through more equitable models of representation. Representation theory proffers ways of understanding the relationship between representation and the represented from both the normative and empirical perspectives (Pitkin, 1967; Philipps, 1994; Lovenduski & Norris, 1993; 1995; Norris & Lovenduski, 1995; Powell Jr., 2004; Pitkin (1967) differentiates representatives' objectives on the pendulum between political tasks and constituency expectations. As she argues, an over-emphasis on the composition of political bodies prevents a proper focus on the activity of representation; in her view, it is more important to focus on what representatives do than on who they are. This is also behind the yearning for what is considered normal among the interview partners of this study—with less emphasis on their migration backgrounds and more on political practice—since they face the expectation of representing migrant community (Wüst, 2011). However, as the analytical findings demonstrate it is not possible to neglect their background completely; more significantly this reluctance is not as consistent, if one solely considers the strategy of redefinition. Furthermore, the strategy of political diversification demarcates the border between what the interviewed politicians do and who they are. Indeed, who they are specifically refers to their migration backgrounds and is applicable to what politicians do as well as what they are reluctant to do.

Representation model has also influenced studies in the role of women and gender in politics, which has facilitated the ascendancy of representation studies where there is no concrete electoral arrangement for minorities. In those studies, scholars (Philipps, 1995; Mansbridge, 1999; 2004) argued that interest is not only carried by political parties but also via the representatives themselves, and the presence of specific groups reinforces the representation of their interests. While this complementary approach includes the perspectives of the representatives, there is still an important gap in the argument that has to be pinpointed. This is the fact that both studies on the role of race and ethnicity in studies on the role of gender in representation are driven by the common premise that these groups are homogenous units with similar interests, a common identity and clearcut pathways of representation. The assumption is thus that representatives from earlier mentioned groups can and will represent these groups' interests specifically (see also Mansbridge, 1999). These perceived commonalities may be made up of visible characteristics or shared experiences. In other words, descriptive representation argues that "*Being one of us*" is assumed to promote loyalty to "*our interests*" (Mansbridge, 1999: 629). Suffice to say, being one of them is a shortcut identification for politicians, as this study has also evinced; identification fosters an emotional bond rather than a sense of political responsibility. Only if it is seen as a political responsibility does it appear empirically possible to identify whether elected politicians act on the interests of their clientele, as measured through the examination of roll call, legislative initiatives, and other parliamentary tools used by elected officials. But, in the line with Mansbridge (1999), relying on a descriptive representation is attended with the danger of essentialising the "*identity that all members of that group share and of which no others can partake*" (Mansbridge, 1999: 637).

Furthermore, such an assumption also paves the way for a corollary that these elected politicians cannot represent other groups adequately, remaining restricted to the group that with which they share a descriptive trait. The latter aspect in particular is a main concern for the politicians scrutinised in this study and leads to efforts to differentiate their political ambitions from those of migrants in order to escape the '*lobbyist*' label. Mansbridge and like-minded scholars are aware of the danger of essentialism and thus develop alternative research objectives that concentrate on the nature of representation, which is conceptualised in less rigid terms than descriptive representation. Others such as Mary Crawford (2008) concentrate on gendered mechanisms in legislative bodies and examine how these are exercised, in the case of her research, towards female members of the parliament in Australia.

It is still safe to claim that politicians with migration backgrounds in Germany, as well as in many other Western European countries, constitute the exception rather than the rule. This is indicative of the continued tension that they will be conceived as descriptive representatives for migrants, whereas they themselves consider their migration backgrounds to be a visible but not inevitable component of their political identities. Findings from this study suggest that being marked as the descriptive representatives of migrant communities is a sign that their political competence is considered suspect, and that they are considered one among a homogenous mass. This reduction, in turn, creates a perception of stigmatisation as if their competences of representation were diminished. Hence speaking to politicians with migration background attributing them the representation of migrants is seen as an appreciation of their experiences rather than as a priori political task to be fulfilled. They do not engage in politics to represent migrants, except in a few cases, but they do also represent them. Considering this, the interviewed politicians highlighted the compatibility of their skills and beliefs with those of their parties and considered themselves to be building bridges between political bodies and migrant communities. The empirical investigation for this study unrevealed important insights, which together resulted in a more focused research question.

Consequently, the intriguing question as it has evolved has been not whether and how these politicians are recruited, and to what extent they represent the groups assigned to them. This question evolved because interviewees were less concerned about recruitment patterns and the substantive or descriptive representation of migrants, and more concerned about negotiating the role of migration background in the political arena. Informed by the elements of grounded theory data collection and analytical methods, this study has thus focused on how politicians with migration backgrounds negotiate their marker of difference while serving in the parliaments of Germany.

For this reason, the study went on to examine how representation is exercised when politicians were not elected specifically to represent one demographic subgroup, but still carry the mark of one of these subgroups. In this respect, the marker of difference took on a multidimensional character in the research that swung between stigma and status. Interesting about these shifting meanings is the remarkable management strategies embedded within them, especially taking into account that people with migration backgrounds have been either viewed negatively because of their marker or described as success stories in spite of it. The marker presents itself in a genuinely multifaceted and multifunctional way for the people concerned.

In order to crystallise the continuous intermingling of statements between status and stigma, this study has utilised the concept of stigma management by Erving Goffman (1959; 1963) as a heuristic tool in the analysis. The literature on disadvantaged groups in political representation discussed in this study have underlined that there is no single social meaning attached to the marker of difference in the practice of politics. Through analysis of the divergent social meanings observed in various contexts, this study has uncovered the net of intertwined meanings deployed over the course of their political careers, and has pinpointed two main limitations to the notion of stigma as developed by Goffman. In contrast to conventional understandings of stigma, which consider it to be a generally negative and inevitable status, this study has shown that associations with migration background spans from one pole to the other. The actors, who are involved actively, transform the meaning based on context, position and sphere of influence. To put it another way, while interviewees with upper middle- class backgrounds and degrees from higher education institutions often distanced themselves ability and cultural competency were recognised, they were embraced by the same interviewees. Patterns of handling these connotations were also marked by ambivalence.

The analysis distilled five main themes inflating into the management of the marker, titled as strategies. These themes are:

neutralisation, redefinition, compensation, singularisation, and political diversification. To sustain their political careers, interviewed politicians deploy various strategies with various audiences and regarding various issues. Next, there are logical bonds connecting each theme. The analysis starts off with the political interest and legislative recruitment phases, wherein the marker is mainly positioned towards party delegates and political aspirants with or without migration backgrounds, whereas at the second stage the marker of diversity is presented within a political environment as these elected representatives address the electorate on behalf of the party. This latter phase differs from the first as the marker is deployed more readily in political practice. Subsequent phases balance political practice between the negative connotation and advantages gained by the marker. Hence, strategies provide more insight than the sum of each strategy, this study provides an excellent opportunity to fill the apparent gap in the literature on how politics is exercised with the marker migration backgrounds.

Indeed, management of the marker of migration background in politics is reinforced by the zealous orientation of politicians towards success, as this study has shown. This makes the marker a dynamic and contextually conditioned characteristic. Neutralisation strategy, refers to the importance of the interviewees' skills to their ability to access political channels. Especially at this stage, the marker is an apparent but negligible factor in nomination, and it is interesting to note that politicians attach little to no significance to background retrospectively, even though most of them cited it in their speeches at the party delegates' conference. This crystallises the marker as a stigmatised achievement that has to be carefully formulated in political existence, since representation is predicated on the fight to win majorities. Still, the non-influential role granted to social background in legislative recruitment becomes a resource for both non-migrant politicians and for political rivals with migration backgrounds. In later career phases, strategic deployment of the marker as a resource is used in particular among parties with fewer representatives of migration background in order to attract support by means of the identifier 'I am one of them'; that is, through language or cultural brokerage roles. Regardless of the price paid in the past for this privileged status among migrants, this mode of management is exemplified as a compensation strategy in this study. Compensation strategies involve sometimes working many times harder than needed, but this is not articulated through the language of victimisation, which would have characterised the circumstances resulting in the strategy as a matter of destiny. For this reason, compensation strategies result in a respect for achievements rather than blame for shortcomings, which would contradict with neutralisation strategy. Among the politicians in this study, this demonstrates why and how success has been achieved to anyone who doubts such political positions can be earned, and who suspects they have been gifted by virtue of the marker.

Another important pan-strategic factor is the societal role politicians adopt; in emphasising this, respondents draw a line between so-called typical migrants and migrant elites. It is among the upwardly mobile that these politicians count themselves, with the dividing line being drawn along educational and/or occupational status. Many interviewees stressed that little public attention has been paid to these positive cases among migrant communities, and through their public visibility this is apt to change and thus foster integration. Besides adopting a role in societal transformation within the framework of the strategies demarcated in this research, such an approach also hints at redefinition of the marker through an enhancement of differences.

Politicians with migration backgrounds have exhibited a range of modes for managing the shadows that threaten to simultaneously harm and benefit their political careers. Within these strategies, the mission is to control the marker in such a way as to have their achievements respected. The boundaries between the various contextual associations of the marker offer a rich resource regarding the creation of policies as well as the ammunition to destroy it if overused. While in political office the deployment of the marker has to be such that the politician has room to be free of it as well, since, notwithstanding the fact that yearning for normality collides with the dominant argument that their political presence is not extraordinary in and of itself. This leaves the research question open as to how this normality can be achieved lies in the numerical increase of politicians with migration backgrounds. Furthermore, the transformative level, meaning changes in the perception, exposed roles and functions that respondents self-defined as being partly dependent on the fact that there are not so many politicians with migration backgrounds; consequently, normality would mean the end of some or all of these functions and roles, too. It is claimed that strategic support for numeric increase may result in the prioritisation of background over political skills, which would load the marker with negative meaning. Here the negative load is the implication that migrants are dependent on assistance, making them victims. Taking into account that political actors with migration backgrounds themselves oppose systematic assistance, an increase in the number of parliamentarians with migration backgrounds is thus left to the course of events in the foreseeable future.

Conclusion

In this articles elaborated how member of parliaments with migration backgrounds in Germany negotiate their marker of diversity. This implied a focus on the role of migration background in their career biographies, from party affiliation to electoral candidacy and present position. Participating members of parliament (MPs), taking a retrospective journey through their political careers positioned and contextualised the issue of migration background in political practice.

In this sense the findings of this research reversed earlier approaches to the question "what difference markers make in politics" (Swain, 1993), asking instead how the marker can be deployed in order not to make a difference.

Accordingly three main conclusions can be articulated. First, contrary to expectations, politicians from different parties have shown relatively similar patterns in how they perceived and negotiated their marker, migration background. Second, all interviewees put a greater emphasis on their German identity, strengthened by a border drawing process from undesired image of people with migration background in Germany. This process of differentiation relies mainly on educational achievement and language competencies, which constitute the main point of critic against migrants. Particularly this aspect provides an important clue that the marker is externally negatively loaded and there is an urge on part of politicians to avoid this negative connotation. The combination of migration background and political identity in fact triggers strategies for management of the marker that aim at deploying it in a positive light in order to avoid the underestimation of the marker. Third, all politicians were inclined to assign less emphasis to the marker at the recruitment stage, as opposed to the period as elected politicians. At subsequent stages the marker is presented as a resource rather than an impediment. This finding implies that the marker is a source of ambivalence for politicians; it may be a stigma when understood in relation to negative images of the marker, but it may also be a rich resource when supported by distinguishing elements such as political talent, language proficiency, and educational profile together with the diversity marker. Furthermore, the interplay between stigma and resource within management strategy have conveyed that this ambivalence will remain as long as the marker is still meaningful for the external audience, or to use interviewees' terms, until normality takes over.

Management of the marker is of importance to the participants of this study because the all politicians with migration backgrounds are confronted almost daily with their social backgrounds in both positive and negative ways. Participants reflected on what kinds of roles migration background as a marker has played and still plays in their political practice, how these practices are perceived, and why it cannot be regarded as exclusively positive or negative. In doing this, they provided invaluable and usually unattainable insights on political practice and logic; this unprecedented candor was made possible through a guarantee of anonymity. Their perspectives shed also light on that migration background is not considered as a homogenous marker, and certain country of origins are seen more relevant for negative connotations as others. Particularly Turkey origin politicians are comprehended as belonging to this latter group due to the dominance in the population.

The study opted to earmark that political practice with a marker is a see-saw that is defined contextually with a continuous negotiation. However, the fact that this is described as being context dependent should not leave the impression that interviewees' accounts contain an inconsistent and fragmented picture of their experiences in the political field. Instead this gives a picture of how diversity markers in an immigration country.

Chapter 6: How Berlin's local politicians of Turkish background perceive their access to party networks and ability to succeed?

Floris Vermeulen and Ayten Doğan

For immigrants and their offspring, being incorporated into the local political system of a European city is in many respects an uphill battle. Newcomers and their descendants do not feature prominently among Europe's parliamentarians or city councillors (Bloemraad, 2013; Bloemraad and Schönwälder, 2013). Political parties seem to have difficulty adapting to the new demographics in which people of immigrant background comprise a large percentage of the city population – or in some cases, like that of Amsterdam, even form the majority. The absence of immigrants from political institutions does not seem to be just an innocent reflection of their recent arrival or slow acquisition of citizenship. More likely we feel it reflects the inability of existing political institutions to adapt to a changing demographic situation.

Michon and Vermeulen (2013) proposed a model for the political incorporation of immigrants that is based on three elements. First, features of the electoral and political systems determine if – and, if so, to what extent – immigrants can vote and get elected. Second, the structure of immigrant groups influences in how far members are able to seize opportunities, which, in turn, affects the extent to which immigrants get elected and become represented constituencies. Third, because parties and their elites choose whether or not to exploit the resources of a given community, it is these power wielders, who facilitate the political participation of immigrants. These factors leave politicians of immigrant background to navigate through an uncertain, often hostile environment, where at any given point their ethnicity may prove an asset – adding diversity to the political party and giving it greater appeal to fellow immigrant voters – or an unequivocal handicap in accessing the corridors of power (Bloemraad, 2013). We hope to better assess that struggle by analysing the current situation in Berlin.

Like most European capitals, Germany has become a diverse nation with many people of immigrant backgrounds. But the city is also home to the largest Turkish immigrant community in Europe with many immigrant organisations (Vermeulen, 2008; Vermeulen, 2013). In this paper, we will describe how Berlin's politicians of Turkish background perceive their position in the local political system. We do this by summarising the respondents' perceptions regarding two important issues: 1) the nature and function of personal networks in political parties; 2) the role ethnicity plays in an individual becoming a successful politician in Berlin. Successful in the sense that politicians themselves feel that they are equally able as politicians without immigration background to have a voice in important discussions, run for office, gain influential political positions, or to be able to influence the party position in important and sensitive political debates. The question this paper seeks to answer is: '*What perceptions do Berlin's politicians of Turkish background hold when it comes to their positioning in the local political system and the extent to which their immigrant background impacts this?*'

Data

To collect our research data, we began by identifying politicians of Turkish background across different political parties in Berlin. Those who have a mandates in one of Berlin's district councils (Bezirksamt) or the House of Representatives (Abgeordnetenhaus). We were able to identify 27 politicians of Turkish background who held a position in one of the councils of Berlin. Furthermore, we included a category of nonpartisan but still politically active respondents with sway over political happenings in Berlin; to create this group, we asked respondents after each interview to refer us to others they thought would be relevant. In total, we conducted approximately one-hour-long semi-structured interviews with 15 politicians: six from the Social Democratic Party (Sozialdemokratische Partei Deutschlands, SPD), four from the Green Party (Bündnis 90/Die Grünen), two from the Left Party (Die Linke), one from the Christian Democratic Union (Christlich Demokratische Union Deutschlands, CDU) and two who were nonpartisans in the period March 2013 to October 2013.

In selecting interviewees, we endeavoured to keep our sample balanced in terms of gender, party, position within party and district. We began by approaching potential respondents at the borough council and from there, we asked interviewees to share their contacts of other politicians of Turkish background. Though it took time, this method facilitated our access to the respondents. In general, politicians from all parties were very cooperative, keen to participate and share their opinions. Some respondents were harder to reach than others due to their demanding position within the party or a lack of time. Out of the 16 potential respondents we contacted, only one refused to do an interview. All interviews were conducted and transcribed in German, excerpts of the interviews used in this paper were translated by the authors.

Germany's political parties and immigrants

During the most recent national elections in 2013, the inclusion and incorporation of the immigrant population in Germany into the political system was a major issue. As Kösemen (2013) states, migrants are becoming more and more valuable as potential voting constituencies. At the same time, however, it is becoming increasingly difficult for parties to maintain such votes since migrants' electoral behaviour is losing predictability. Furthermore, it is difficult for parties to assess the consequences of a particular party position or including representatives of immigrant background on their non-migrant electoral consituency.

Of all the parties, says Kösemen (2013), the CDU has undergone the most profound agenda realignment vis-à-vis migrant politics, making itself more attractive to immigrant voters. This is quite striking seeing as for many years the CDU straddled two positions on migrant politics: benevolent paternalism and defensive ignorance. All the while, progressive voices and proponents of reorienting the party towards integration and migration were isolated internally. On the other hand, it is also clear that to this day, the CDU is the party with the most problematic access for politicians of immigrant background; their representation is still significantly lower than in left-wing parties.

Traditionally, the SPD had been the party with the strongest link to the immigrant constituency. Thilo Sarrazin, however, changed a lot of that single-handedly. The prominent SPD politician, widely criticised for his views on Muslims in Germany, authored Deutschland schafft sich ab ('Germany is doing itself in'). The book, published in 2010, tied a foreign infiltration of German society to the country's Muslim population, who, according to Sarrazin, are unwilling to integrate. SPD borough mayor Heinz Buschkowsky made similar points in Neukölln ist uberall ('Neukölln is everywhere'), published in 2012. Its title referring to one of Berlin's immigrant neighbourhoods, the book correlated immigration with low educational levels, high poverty and high rates of criminal behaviour. Buschkowsky drew on local examples to make generalisations, giving the impression that his analysis of Neukölln was applicable to other parts of Germany as well. Kösemen (2013) states that the Sarrazin case revealed just how high the SPD considered the political costs of a profound rectification of the heated public discussion concerning the book and ensuing damage in relation to its immigrant constituencies.

The Greens are by far the most migrant-friendly, both in terms of party ideology and individual members. At 8.8%, the number of MPs of immigrant background in the Green parliamentary group exceeds the number for all other parties: 8% for the Lefts, 3.4% for the SPD, 2.2% for the FDP and 0.4% for the CDU/CSU (Kösemen, 2013). What is particularly striking about the Greens is the equal percentage of highly educated voters among migrants and non-migrants. Both constituencies fit in the same category: educated, young or middle-aged, urban, well-established, middle-class.

Respondents' descriptions of Berlin's parties were consistent with our understanding of them at the national level. Interviewees also emphasised how all parties have recently begun discovering the immigrant vote. According to one SPD politician:

Nowadays, all parties are positioning themselves on issues that are important to voters with a migrant background. I cannot think of any party that doesn't. The individual issues and questions are well defined in the political arena, and parties are visibly positioning themselves on those issues, particularly during elections and campaigning time. Which party supports dual citizenship? Which party supports municipal suffrage? And, in fact, the very fact and process of positioning during the electoral run-up reveals the importance of those issues for parties.

Respondents also mentioned how political parties in Berlin cater to specific subgroups in the city's large, diverse Turkish community. As this respondent from the SPD (respondent 2) stated:

The Left are doing a lot with Kurdish people. So if you are a Kurd, and preferably a woman too, as well as quite smart, it'll definitely work to your advantage [if you want to be on their list]. [...] In the past, the Greens were also doing a lot with the Kurdish people, but then they preferred to shift [their orientation] towards the Alevis.

A Left respondent (respondent 3) commented on how political parties become more visibly engaged when it comes to immigrant issues during elections, saying:

I don't think that the major parties genuinely support these positions – that is the crux of the matter. They take up issues and questions in order to gather votes from those migrants holding German passports, but they do not translate them into policies afterwards.

Parties' decreased post-election activity around these issues also seems to be a result of people of immigrant background in Berlin being less politically active than other groups when it comes to local issues. An SPD respondent (respondent 2) illustrated the situation as follows:

As an example, let's take the Tempelhofer field, which is a major issue in Berlin. More or less 50% of the residents around the Tempelhofer field have a migrant background. But I have never seen a single one at any event there. I have been at every single event because our district borders the field and our committees are thus involved in those events. There are only white Germans. [...] The migrants' non-interest is remarkable. But the reason for this is not that migrants are too dumb or simply apolitical – it is about participation.

Respondents agreed that political parties, especially larger ones, can no longer ignore issues that are of importance specifically to immigrant constituencies. In a changing Berlin, more diverse than ever, parties have to keep up their image, part of which is determined by the extent to which they represent the changing population. But, as one of the SPD respondents (respondent 2) found, many political parties in Berlin still fail in that regard:

I mean, look, the SPD is 150 years old and there has never been someone with a migrant background on the executive board. We have one who is half-American or half-Austrian or something at the moment. But I think it is kind of offensive, personally speaking, if they say, "We actually do have someone with a migrant background on the board," because those people have no primary physical characteristics [that suggest they are of immigrant background] and are therefore not stigmatised – they are not victims of racism and discrimination.

Another respondent from the SPD (respondent 1) addressed this issue as follows:

I think the time has come for the party to change. What kind of message are we conveying to the public if the SPD hasn't got a single member with a migrant background on the BVV [Bezirksverordnetenversammlung (borough assembly)]? Parties want to win elections and people look at a party in a different way if they have people with migrant backgrounds on their boards and voters then say: "Well, there are people who would represent my interests in the BVV and therefore I'll vote for them."

Politicians and personal party networks

Adding up the narratives of different respondents, one thing is clear: being a successful politician means having sufficiently supportive, influential connections in political parties. Almost all respondents cited these networks as crucial, as their main tool for gaining access to parties. One of the Green respondents (respondent 6) formulated it like this:

What you need is support. I couldn't do it on my own. What I have realised and learned during my work is that you always need other people. Whether you want to improve yourself or to progress, you'll always need people who support you since you can never do it on your own. You need people in your parliamentary group who tell you: "Yes, we'll support you. Keep on trying. Run for that post. You can do it!" Everything will be much easier this way. But if people tell you, "Nope, we won't support you," then nothing will work out – all you need is support.

Most respondents saw this as a natural part of being a politician. Moreover, they found it unrelated to their personal backgrounds and even comparable to the situation in which other politicians in the system would find themselves. As this SPD (respondent 8) respondent put it:

You will have to build your own networks – though that is particularly difficult if you regularly move from one place to another. You will have to engage in what I would describe as a 'practice of petitions'. You will have to stand out from the crowd in terms of your ideas, but at the same time you will have to attract majorities – showing individual qualities within the party, in particular, but also innate political skills, in general.

Networks as such must include influential party members who provide access to relevant positions within the party. Most often, these individuals have no immigrant background themselves. It was striking that very few respondents cited Turkish networks or Turkish organisations as a means to access the party. As we also heard in our interviews, a heavy reliance on personal ties with political elites often leaves young politicians vulnerable. Losing a crucial connection in their network can have negative ramifications for their career future. An SPD respondent (respondent 2) shared this information:

I won't name any particular names here, but there are people who abandoned me. It was the head of the district committee [...]. I don't think that he/she dumped me because he/she didn't like me, but there are simply multiple forces and interests at stake, which led to that abandonment. Well, 'abandoning' may sound a bit harsh, but basically he/she did not support me anymore.

How politicians of Turkish background access the local political system

When inquiring into respondents' perception of how they go about getting access or how frequently they get access, we discussed the extent to which political parties in Berlin were not only willing to address topics of possible importance to an immigrant constituency, but also the extent to which parties were interested in selecting politicians of immigrant background. Overall, respondents cited improvement from the situation in the 1980s and early 1990s. For example, a Left respondent (respondent 3) said:

I think that Germany's political landscape has changed and improved a lot during the last 20 years. Of course, it's not perfect yet, but what can ever be said to be perfect? There are [now] ministers on the federal state level and party leaders with a migrant background who have made it that far. There are MPs, representatives, mayors and many more. [...] I think that all of us have proven that people with a migrant background can also make it to the top in Germany.

Respondents with more experience felt that Berlin had moved into a new phase, one in which a candidate's ethnic background is no longer the most important factor for determining career prospects. An SPD respondent (respondent 15) put it this way:

I think that it is up to the migrants themselves. What kind of interests do they have? What do they think they are capable of achieving? As well as whether there are possibilities and opportunities for them in the party or parliamentary group. But I think that the time when you could easily get involved and climb the ladder in party politics merely because you had a migrant background are over. And to be honest, I think that this is a positive change. Now you have to bring yourself in and, if that works out, you'll succeed and progress.

Another Green respondent (respondent 12) stated the following:

When I am campaigning, all shop owners with a Turkish migrant background pass out my flyers and material, are very friendly and show interest. But the same is true for the German ones. So I cannot say whether my migrant background is working to my advantage. In fact, I cannot even say what role my Turkish background plays at all in my constituency. But I think it makes no difference. Nobody is voting for me just because I was born in Turkey. [...] Personally, I see myself as a German MP and, similar to [my responses to] questions regarding gender politics, I think the glass ceiling is predominantly anchored in one's own thinking.

However, most respondents also admitted that it is still not an easy process. To gain access to a party, politicians of immigrant background struggle more than those who are not of immigrant backgrounds. In fact, some respondents even mentioned an unspoken ranking in which immigrants come last, meaning that politicians of Turkish background who wish to be successful often have to work harder and have more persistence. As this Green respondent (respondent 12) explained it:

There clearly is a pecking order: first men, second women and then the migrants – maybe followed by disabled people, but I am not sure about that. But such pecking orders can be found everywhere in society and the same is true for politics. [...] As there clearly is an inequality between men and women, there also is an inequality between migrants and non-migrants. And if you are a female migrant, you experience double discrimination. Those are matters of fact and their existence cannot be argued away.

Other respondents' conceptualised the ranking differently, feeling that being both female and of immigrant background was not necessarily a double disadvantage. As this SPD member (respondent 2) said:

Being male and having an oriental background is always unfortunate. Don't get me wrong, but I am trying to make a point here. Or having a Muslim background is even worse; you'll have to face so many problems. As a woman, you can always use your Muslim background to act out the victim and rebel role – that's just the way it is and you see it everywhere in politics. For example, 90% of those with a migrant background who are successful in the Green Party are women. That isn't a problem, per se, but the point I am trying to make here is that men, if they are Muslims, are stigmatised in certain ways. But the only way to get rid of the stigmatisation and prejudices is by distancing yourself far from your own cultural background, to the point of almost positioning yourself further to the right than every right-wing populist.

Still, almost all respondents would seemingly agree that whether or not a Berlin politician is of immigrant background impacts the extent to which the individual can be successful, the gender issue notwithstanding. As this SPD member (respondent 15) put it:

I think there certainly is a glass ceiling, which I personally had to experience during my lifetime, too.

Parties often expect politicians of Turkish background to focus only on issues related to immigration and integration. But doing so can have negative effects, precluding a politician from opportunities for growth and promotion within the party, as immigration issues are seldom deemed top priority. The same SPD respondent (respondent 15) explained it as follows:

Well, doing integration politics in Parliament is one thing. Then you are being supported, trusted, and others appreciate your work and effort. But it's totally different if you are running for an executive position within the party. In that case, you cannot expect any support. That was a crucial experience and turning point, when I thought, "So this is how people actually think of you: Migrants should do politics for migrants; but as for all other issues, tasks and positions, the time has not come yet."

Other respondents shared similar perceptions. In their view, personal skills and experience were the most important factors for most politicians, when it came to deciding on which issue they would become a party speaker or expert. But for politicians of immigrant background, this was less the case; parties expected them to focus only on immigration and integration, a tendency greatly frustrating many of the respondents. As a Green member (respondent 9) said:

If you have a different [ethnic] background, what usually happens is that an attributive political classification takes place, like, "Well you can always do migration policies, you don't need any expertise for that." It's the same with women doing gender politics. But this is, I think, an even greater problem in other parties. I guess it's easier to thrust oneself forward into the spotlight on migrant-related topics. But that is such nonsense; everyone has certain expertise, knowledge and experiences. And based on such competences, positions should be assigned, and not based on cultural descents. I think that this is still a major problem in many parties, which I think the Greens are no exception of.

On the other hand, some respondents felt it was meaningful to have someone of immigrant background talk about these subjects because of their first-hand experience with the circumstances of immigrant communities in Berlin. In the words of an SPD (respondent 1) member:

I think it is important that when we talk about migrant politics, migrants be the ones sitting at the table, too. That was in fact my very intention, why I got involved in politics. So many people talk about migration, migrants, religion, Islam – but all those people know nothing about it, or are not affected by those issues at all.

Some respondents disclosed the fact that their personal opinion on integration issues did not always match the position of the party or influential members thereof. This often appeared to be the case among SPD politicians, in particular, whose conflicting interests inevitably led to the politician having to end the discussion or losing any prospects for career advancement in the party. One SPD respondent (respondent 1) described how trying such situations can be, saying:

There are some sensitive topics, like Islam or, well, not being Turkish, per se, but I would say migration, in general. Those are topics that affect me personally – especially when people [including party members] talk about topics that they know nothing about at all or are simply misinformed about. That's when I sometimes get too emotional, which makes it difficult for me to keep calm. Or I'll simply keep my mouth shut and I have to tell myself that I won't argue about that because it simply won't change a thing. There are moments like this, yes.

Another SPD respondent (respondent 2) explained how his explicit stance in the Sarrazin and the Buschkowsky discussions led to his marginal position in the party, recalling:

Looking at the developments during the past two years, I would have to say that I am not really being promoted within the party. People do rather look at me as though I am a problem, which I must admit has to do with my general attitude. I was, for example, one of the people who cried loudest when it came to Sarrazin as well as Buschkowsky.

If we take these experiences as evidence, it does not seem advantageous for politicians of Turkish background to have a clear-cut ethnic constituency. One of the Green respondents (respondent 12) articulated the dilemma as follows:

I think that the stronger your ties to your Turkish background are, the more difficult it is to represent everyone's interests. But my understanding of politics is that you should not become an MP in order to represent Turks, but rather that you be a representative of the people, in the true sense of the word, and hence represent everyone. But from what I sense, there seems to be a generational change towards this issue since, particularly the younger generation take this for granted.

Conclusion

Our research set out to capture present-day perceptions of politicians of Turkish background in Berlin concerning their own positioning in the local political system. This paper first sought to explain to what extent they saw opportunities for themselves to be successful politicians, capable of representing their constituencies. Second, the paper endeavoured to assess perceptions of the extent to which their immigrant background may have played a role in their capacities. From our interviews with 15 of Berlin's 26 local politicians of Turkish background at the time, we got the impression that, more and more, all major political parties in Berlin deem it important to attract voters of Turkish background and that this leads to greater opportunities for politicians of Turkish background. However, such opportunities are mostly found in left-wing parties (SPD, Greens, and die Linke). Moreover, even among these parties, politicians of immigrant background are still relatively few and restricted to comparatively less influential positions. This tendency led some respondents to wonder whether the main political parties are really willing to change and provide opportunities for politicians of immigrant background.

Most respondents stated the importance of personal networks that include influential members without immigration background of their own parties. Without these contacts, they felt unable to be promoted in the party. In addition, lacking such contacts made many of them vulnerable, as the networks were not part of some pre-existing system and had to be actively pursued. Losing a personal contact – for instance, because a politician of Turkish background took a different stance from his or her contact on a particular issue – could have serious, negative consequences for his or her career.

Some respondents felt that their Turkish background was less important for their position in the party than it may have been ten or 20 years ago. They believed politicians were judged on personal merits and not included or excluded because of their ethnic background. However, most of the respondents still perceived a clear pecking order in all of Berlin's major political parties, where being of immigrant background was rarely advantageous to their party career. They cited a common tendency for party members to assume that politicians of Turkish background would be spokespersons for immigration and integration affairs rather than other issues, such as finance and economics. There was also less support from other party members when politicians of immigrant background ran for executive positions in the party. In addition, respondents across parties found it a challenge to take an oppositional stance in debates related to immigration, integration or Islam. These circumstances make it tricky, if not impossible, for politicians possessing a strong connection with the Turkish constituency and representing their opinions in sensitive discussions to become successful, in the sense that people can get executive positions, become influential party members and/or participate visible in sensitive political debates, in any of the major parties in Berlin. From our interviews with politicians, we got the impression that political parties in Berlin are increasingly keen to attract voters of immigrant background – that inclination increases the chance for politicians of Turkish background to gain access to the parties. Nevertheless, parties are often still reluctant to incorporate the opinions and positions of some of these voters and politicians in their programmes. This is most likely because the political parties are afraid that including too many opinions, positions and/or persons from immigrant constituencies will have a negative effect on their non-immigrant electoral basis (Kösemen, 2013).

Chapter 7: After the Hamburg Cell: the Integration Debate and Turkish-German Representation in Post-9/11 Media and Politics

Emily Joy Rothchild

On 11 September 2001, hijacked planes struck the World Trade Center, the Pentagon, and a Pennsylvania field. The attacks horrified people worldwide, but German reactions were especially complicated; politicians and citizens needed to process the failed macro-political integration of the Hamburg cell, four 9/11 conspirators who met and organized at Al-Quds Moschee (mosque). Just one year prior in 2000, citizenship law reform changed the idea of who could be German, one that now included the country's Turkish-German population. Though none of the Hamburg cell members were Turkish, 9/11's temporal closeness to citizenship law reform and the resultant collusion of "Turk" and "Muslim" in media and political discourse resulted in continuing negative media representation of Turkish-Germans.

Particularly since 2001, Germany has struggled with increased Islamophobia, fear of Islam and by association, Muslims. Chancellor Angela Merkel has promoted the creation of integration programs aimed at stopping problems before they start. Nevertheless, migrants often feel they belong *less* when others mark them in need of integration. In this chapter, I ask: how has media representation towards Turkish-Germans changed since 9/11 and citizenship law reform? How has media coverage of Germany's integration crisis impacted migrant descendants' sense of belonging, a key facet of macro-political integration?

I begin my analysis by reviewing literature that charts media representations of Muslims prior to and after 9/11, showing the transition of migrants from Muslim-majority countries appearing in German media sources as Turks, then as foreigners, and later as Muslims. I elucidate the influence of the 2000 citizenship law reform on societal perceptions of Muslims, demonstrating while citizenship status first characterized the in-group/out-group dichotomy, religion took its place. Using *Der Spiegel* as my primary case study, I conduct textual and visual analysis of title articles pertaining to Islam or Muslims to chart the magazine's pre- and post-9/11 descriptions of Muslims from 1999-2011. Lastly, I utilize findings from my 2010-2014 ethnographic research with migrant descendants at the Hamburg HipHop Academy to demonstrate how media and political representations of "*ethnic Muslims*" impact the lives of Turkish-German migrant descendants in Hamburg who confront stereotypes daily. I argue these youths' testimonies of belonging and Germanness contradict media portrayals of "*ethnic Muslims*" and reinforce the need for mutual awareness between Germans, migrants, and their descendants in order to achieve macro-political integration.

The Media's "Ethnic Muslim": Turk, Foreigner, Muslim again

Modern media representation of Muslims can be traced to the post-WWII era. West Germany began hiring Italian *Gastarbeiter* (guestworkers) to fill labour shortages in 1955, but the need for workers hastened and recruitment reached Turkey in 1961. The government viewed these workers as a temporary solution for the country's workforce needs but never intended them to stay and in November 1973, government officials placed a moratorium on guestworker recruitment due to a stagnant economy resulting from the global oil crisis and recession. At the time, 2.6 million *Gastarbeiter* lived in West Germany; 605,000 were Turkish, constituting 23% of non-citizens residing in the nation-state. Family reunification programs began in 1974 and allowed workers' families to join them. Many families followed due to beneficial economic and educational opportunities and the overall population of non-citizens in Germany swelled, reaching 4.4 million by 1980 (Göktürk et al., 2007, p.9-11).

An important factor in media representation of Muslims arose with the retirement of *ius sanguinis*, which limited paths to citizenship for those without "*ethnic German*" heritage. In 2000, Chancellor Gerhard Schröder's Social Democrat (SPD)/Green Party coalition reformatted citizenship law. Dual citizenship became possible until one's 23rd birthday and paths to naturalization eased. Since reform, there has been increasing societal fear of the growing immigrant population from "*ethnic Muslim*" countries accompanying decreasing "*ethnic German*" birth rates. Today, the Turkish community in Germany has surpassed 3.2 million and the population of "*ethnic Muslims*" totals 4 million, comprising 5% of the country's total population of approximately 80.8 million. As the majority of these immigrants are Turkish, "*Muslim*" and "*Turk*" have been conflated in media and political discourse. The fusion of Muslim and Turk encourages a homogenous view of an ethnically and religiously diverse Muslim community. Sunnis comprise Germany's Muslim majority, though Alevis are half a million. Regardless, only 15-20% of Germany's "*ethnic Muslims*" practice Islam regularly (Peter, 2010, p.121).

Before 9/11, nomenclature for "*ethnic Muslims*" was structured around criteria for citizenship and ethnicity; religion was more an assumption than an identifying marker. Though "*Muslim*" could equate "*Turk*," citizen versus non-citizen status was more significant. Labels for the Turkish population included *Migranten* (migrants), *Zuwanderer (*immigrants) or *ausländische Mitbürger (*foreign co-citizens) (ibid. p.127). Citizenship reform prompted a national identity crisis; 200,000-300,000 immigrants naturalize annually and "*ethnic Muslims*" are no longer official outsiders. While before 2000, social problems relating to *Migranten* carried the labels foreigner, migrant, or Turk, these terms no longer apply as migrants have become citizens (Spielhaus, 2006, p.18).

9/11 brought new sensitivity to the religious nature of populations from Muslim-majority countries. The 2004 Madrid bombing prompted Christian Democrat (CDU) and SPD politicians to consider whether their lack of recognition of Islam encouraged the radicalization and alienation of Muslims, ultimately leading to terrorism. The religious motivation of the attacks catalysed rethinking of the nomenclature of Germany's immigrant populations. Conflating ethnicity and religion seemed inappropriate with the presence of a global jihad campaign. Nonetheless, although politicians began to reflect, media sources did not opt for new tactics. Citizenship law change coupled with 9/11 and increased terrorism in Europe catalysed the media's shift from using "*Turk*" or "*foreign*" to substituting the unqualified "*Muslim,*" endowing the term with "*autonomous relevance*" (Peter, 2010, p.127). "*Muslims*" rather than "*Turks*" became the Other or out-group; their label merely changed.

Since 9/11 and the Madrid (2004) and London (2005) bombings, Islamophobia has pervaded Europe. Analysing European leader, media, and citizen responses to the London and Madrid bombings, Fekete (2009) suggests the moral panic that has erupted throughout Europe is indicative of a "*new McCarthyism*" with the Islamic radical replacing the Communist. Shooman and Spielhaus (2007, p.201) attribute the growing fear of Islamization in Germany not just to terrorism but also to the rising number of naturalized Muslims with political agendas. "*Ethnic Germans*'" "*moral panic*" aligns with Appadurai's (2006) "*majoritanism,*" which builds on out-group/in-group designations by suggesting majorities differentiate minorities to create "*we-ness*" because they fear if they do not bond together, they could become a minority. Essentially, if "*ethnic German*" birth rates continue to decline, "*ethnic Muslims*" could become the majority and supplant "*original German*" interests.

In sum, within German media from the 1960s through today, "*ethnic Muslims*" have shifted from being "*Turks*" or "*foreigners*" to becoming generic Muslims sans ethnic specification. Always, the Muslim is the Other, belonging to the out-group in opposition to the "*ethnic German*" in-group. Integration efforts—which I discuss later in this chapter—that receive media notice reconfirm there is a problem in need of solving.

Der Spiegel and Islam: Pre- and Post-9/11 Media Representations of Muslims

Der Spiegel, translated as "*The Mirror*," is a German national newsmagazine published in Hamburg with a weekly circulation over one million. Its online website *Spiegel Online* has high readership due to cost-free access to the majority of its articles. *Spiegel Online* saw 9.97 million unique users/month in 2011—a figure totalling over 12% of the national population. The potential influence of *Der Spiegel* on public opinion towards *Migranten* is tied to its target demographic: high-earning, educated, urban-dwelling elites. *Spiegel Online* has the largest share of these populations among major daily and weekly German news sources. 19.6% of high earners, 20.4% of urban-dwelling elites, and 17.7% of young educated elites choose *Spiegel Online* as their online news source. Readers use *Spiegel Online* especially for the *Politik* (politics) section, which receives 3.6 million unique visitors/month. The role of *Spiegel Online* has intensified over the last decade with page clicks increasing steadily and spiking during times of crisis, e.g. the Iraq War or the Fukushima nuclear disaster (2011, p.7-10). For this analysis, I focus on title/feature/cover articles, those publicized on the magazine cover and normally constituting four to nine thousand words. These articles are available online at no cost and thus are likely to have a large readership. Furthermore, because the magazine's covers feature these articles, the topics could stimulate someone to purchase the magazine from a newsstand.

On 2 June 2001, *Der Spiegel*'s cover asked, "Wer war Mohammed?" (Who was Mohammed?). Attempting to uncover "Das Geheimnis des Islam" (The Secret of Islam), the issue features a twelve-page title article "Die Macht des Propheten" (The Power of the Prophet). Author Follath begins with othering language. He notes the West has watched warily as Islam has grown and prognosticates whether holy war is a threat. He writes no world religion but Islam is so foreign to *us*, or as dynamic, or demands so much from its believers and gives them so much. Through his use of "*us*", Follath immediately "*others*" Muslims, casting them to out-group status, apart from *Der Spiegel*'s presumably non-Muslim, "*ethnic German*" readers (Follath, 2001, p.158).

Though Follath asks whether the Prophet Muhammad preached tolerance, images of bomb-strapped Lebanese fighters and burqa-clad Afghani women imply Islam is *not* a religion of peace but rather one of terror and oppression. A map showing the percentage of Muslims per country has red-coloured icons that resemble both minarets and missiles—the more Muslims, the higher the minaret or the longer the missile (ibid., p.160). The display of images combined with Follath's questioning aligns with meaning-induction: one sees texts juxtaposed with images without explicit justification but with high potential for suggestiveness (Schiffer, 2008, p.430).

Although Follath provides information about the life and tellings of Muhammad, he focuses more heavily on Hamas, Hezbollah, and fighters in Bosnia. The message of the graphics and texts is Islam and terrorism are spreading. His last enlarged text demands: "*Der Islam muss zwischen Taliban und Reformern entscheiden, zwischen Terror und Toleranz*" (the Islam must decide between Taliban and reformers, between terror and tolerance), which begs the question, tolerance of what? Of Christians and Jews, of Western ideals? This decision does not belong to Islam but to individual Muslims. By addressing Islam as a single entity, Follath ignores the vast diversity of Islamic interpretations and teachings. He states terrorists abuse the ideals of God yet argues Muhammad has a place in the modern world, but with this pictorial representation and stories of terror, a world with Muhammad's inspiration appears like one Germans should fear.

Plentiful fear arrived with the news of the Hamburg cell's involvement in 9/11. Germany's second largest city with 1.799 million residents, Hamburg has been at the crossroads of local and international exchange since the founding of its port on the Elbe River in 1189. Like other cities in the former West Germany, Hamburg welcomed *Gastarbeitern*, and today's community of Muslims has grown due to later migrations from Iran and Afghanistan. Hamburg has an active, diverse Muslim population with forty-one mosques and a regular attendance of 11,359 worshipers at Friday prayer services (Moscheen in Hamburg, 2013). 130,000 identified Muslims and 50,000 self-reported Alevis together comprise over 10% of Hamburg's population (*Spiegel Online,* 2012). 29.2% of Hamburgers have a migration background. Hamburg cell members congregated in districts having larger than average immigrant populations. 49.6% of residents from the city district Harburg, where the cell members lived, and 36.6% of residents from Sankt Georg, the Middle Eastern district home to many mosques including the former Al-Quds, have migration backgrounds (Regionalergebnisse, 2011).

Responding to 9/11, *Der Spiegel* published a series of title articles questioning how the Hamburg cell could have perpetrated the attacks. The 26 November 2001, 9,447-word article with the title "Die Krieger aus Pearl Harburg" (The fighters from Pearl Harbour) connects Harburg to Pearl Harbor and signals trouble and impending war. Text centres on terror: *Terrorpiloten* (terror pilots), *Massenmörder* (mass murderers), *Terrorzelle* (terror cell), *Attentat* (assassin), and *Attentäternetzwerks* (Assassins network). Authors tie cell members to bin Laden and his *Heiligen Krieg* (Holy War), comparing the cell's Marienstraße 54 apartment to bin Laden's

Afghani and Pakistani training camps (Brinkbäumer et al., 2001, p.40).

Mohammad Atta, the plot's Egyptian leader and pilot of AA Flight 11, UA Flight 175 Emirati pilot Marwan al-Shehhi, and UA Flight 93 Lebanese pilot Ziad Jarrah first appear in Brinkbäumer et al.'s article as "German" cell members with no indication of their national origins, despite none of the men having German citizenship. Additionally, none of these men was Turkish yet the media's oft-conflation of Muslim and Turk accompanied by no other clarification creates room for readers' speculation or assumption of the cell members' national origins.

In the piece, the authors delve into the men's personalities and backgrounds. They suggest no one could have known or was to blame for allowing these men to do their work largely unnoticed. When the pilots came to Hamburg, they were: "*Junge Leute, Muslime natürlich und fleißige Studenten, deshalb Musterbeispiele für die Integrationsfähigkeit dieser Gesellschaft*" (Young people, Muslims of course and diligent students, therefore prime examples for the integration potential of this society) (Brinkbäumer et al., 2001, p.43). Notable in this description is the authors mentioning that the men were "*Muslims of course.*" Jarrah is from Lebanon where over 40% of the population is Christian; the construction of all people from Muslim-majority countries as Muslim is errant but aligns with Frank Peter (2010)'s suggestion that post-9/11 conditions focused on the autonomous Muslim irrespective of ethnic affiliation or citizenship status.

Each cell member's biography has a common trajectory of immigration, education, and radicalization (Brinkbäumer et al., 2001). The cell members adhered to the top qualifications both European Union citizens and migrants expressed were necessary for social integration in the May 2011 European Commission's Qualitative Eurobarometer report on Migrant Integration: *lingua franca* mastery, education, job acquisition, and adherence to social norms (Migrant Integration, 2011, p. 49-77). The irony of 9/11 and resultant integration initiatives is that the 9/11 pilots *were* educated, German-speaking, legal, seemingly *integrated* migrants but despite their ideal profiles, they still became terrorists. They were "*good*" migrants and "*good*" Muslims, yet 9/11 still happened. As a result, their

"*Muslimness*" more than any other trait has remained in the public mind and has resulted in greater restrictions on migration (Modood et al., 2006, pp.1, 10).

During the year following 9/11, *Spiegel Online* page clicks steadily increased and in 2002, the magazine's focus remained on the terrorists with a pair of articles devoted to the cell and its Germany-based affiliates (*Spiegel Online,* 2011, p.7). After 2002, articles relating to Muslims centred on the U.S. war in Iraq, the German deployment in Afghanistan and updates on the capture of German Al-Qaeda affiliates. Since Germany downplayed its role in Iraq, the war received less coverage than other issues regarding Muslims, such as homeland security and the on-going need for the macro-political integration of migrants and their descendants.

On 29 September 2003, *Der Spiegel* published a fifteen-page commentary on Afghan-German Fereshta Ludin's headscarf controversy titled "Das Kreuz mit dem Koran" (The Cross with the Qur'an), suggesting Ludin's desire to veil as a schoolteacher amounted to her wanting to be treated better than others and because millions of Muslim women do not veil, the headscarf acts as a flag for Islamic fundamentalism. Questioning how much tolerance a western European nation can have without losing its identity, authors stress "*frauenfeindlichen*" (misogynistic) Islamic fundamentalists go against autonomy, prizing collective over individual rights (Cziesche et al., 2003, p.85-86).

Throughout the article, Cziesche et al. did not present any benefits of veiling. Instead, they strove to "*mirror*" public opinion while driving it through rhetoric. The authors use public opinion data to reason why wearing headscarves is counterproductive to integration and female empowerment. In a survey of 1,000 respondents, 38% believed women in civil service should be allowed to veil; 53% disagreed (ibid., p.85). More pointedly, the magazine polled Muslims of Turkish origin, only 27% of whom stated Muslim women should veil in public (ibid., p.90). While Turkish Muslims—especially Alevis—tend to be more secular than Muslims of other origin in Germany, the authors use Turkish opinions to justify veiling is unnecessary for believers and a sign of looming Islamization that threatens integration.

Cziesche et al. warned against fundamentalism through shocking words, terms, and images that became more prevalent in the 2003-2011 period. Major terrorist attacks spawned additional feature articles but these rarely focused on the event; rather they examined the domestic situation and threatening Islamization. Recurrent news stories regarding Muslims over the last several years have focused on the persistent struggle of integration and opposing politicians' jibes. CDU politician Rita Süssmuth, former head of the Immigration Commission of the Federal Government, admitted for years that return rather than integration was the goal. Tolerance was the *raison d'etre* but there was little encouragement for migrants to adapt to German customs (Brandt et al., 2004).

Politicians have contributed to Islamization fears, throwing political correctness to the wayside and generating media notice. A recent wave of Islamophobia traces to 2010 when Thilo Sarrazin published his bestseller *Deutschland schafft sich ab* (Germany does away with itself). This book coupled with CSU leader Horst Seehofer suggesting Germany allow no more Arab or Turkish immigrants due to their difficulties adapting to "*Germany's way of life*" brought to surface latent tension surrounding Muslims (Walker, 2010). Merkel added her voice to the fray, proclaiming "*Der Ansatz für Multikulti ist gescheitert, absolut gescheitert!*" (The approach for multiculturalism has failed, absolutely failed!) (Integrationsdebatte, *Spiegel Online*, 2010). A Gallup Muslim-West Relations Survey reflects the shift in public opinion during this time. In 2008, 65% of Germans believed the West respected Muslim countries, a figure falling to 56% in 2011 after the Islamophobia resurgence (*Gallup,* 2011). At the time of writing, Islamophobia in Germany has surged again due to German-based fighters contributing to the Islamic State's brutal attempt to establish an Islamic caliphate in Syria and Iraq. About 300 jihadis, or 0.0075% of Germany's "*ethnic Muslims*," travelled to fight but their stories are the ones *Der Spiegel* tells (Greene & Torre, 2014; Schrep, 2014).

Opinion polls and surveys from 2009 reflect a country already facing negative feelings towards immigrants. In a survey, although 69% of immigrants felt comfortable in Germany with 58% feeling part of German society, "*ethnic Germans*'"reception of non-Christian residents was lukewarm (*Bertelsmann-Stiftung*, 2009). A Volkswagen

Stiftung-sponsored study further showed only 49% of West Germans and 53% of East Germans were ready to give adherents of non-Christian religions equal rights. This compares to 73% of Danes, 86% of French, 82% of Dutch, and 89% of Portuguese respondents. Additionally, among respondents from all surveyed countries, 80% connected Islam with discrimination towards women, 70% with fanaticism, 60% with violence, and 50% with intellectual bigotry. In Germany, 72% of surveyed West Germans and 69% of East Germans saw the growing diversity of religions as a threat to social peace with only 34% of West Germans and 26% of East Germans holding a positive image of Islam (Bade, 2013, p.18).

For *Der Spiegel,* Marcel Rosenbach and Holger Stark's 2011 article describes the current situation. After 9/11, Turkish-German migrant descendants allegedly had a moderate interpretation of Islam and therefore were less vulnerable to Sunni extremism but today, radical youth go unnoticed (p.33). These statements epitomize the "*good*" versus "*bad*" Muslim dichotomy present in *Der Spiegel*'s coverage of Muslims, warning Germans to stay vigilant. Bruno Schrep's (2014, p.38) exposé on Ahmed K., a Hamburg-born, "*junge Türke*" (young Turk) whose non-veiled, "*westlich*" (western)-clothed aunt thwarted his attempt to fight for the Islamic State, provides a perfect example of a "*good*" Muslim saving the "*bad,*" radicalized, migrant, Muslim youth. Nevertheless, throughout this overview of more than a decade, caution is the resounding cry with images of the "*bad*" Muslim outnumbering mentions of the "*good.*"

Future media and political representation of "*good*" Muslims depends on the role of Germany's Muslims in self-representing the non-violent aspects of their faith and community and on the success of integration efforts. Good self-representation of an out-group is difficult because much self-representation appears defensive against the agenda-setting in-group and any efforts of self-promotion can be perceived as reactive or aggressive (Schiffer, 2008, p.436). Even so, without Muslims' significant effort to self-promote, little improvement will be made and much progress is necessary. As the 2011 Gallup survey indicates, German opinions on the need for good relations with Muslim countries have decreased during a time of increased media exposure regarding the failure of social integration.

Conclusion

Unfortunately, negative media attention towards "*ethnic Muslims*" affects the daily lives of migrant descendants and can stimulate negative counter responses that generate extremism. To counteract perceived integration problems, the German government has attempted to reach its migrant population through integration programs such as language and cultural awareness courses and artistic programming. Through integration language courses, which include sixty hours of mandatory cultural education, the government desires to instil a sense of belonging in immigrants and prevent future attacks (Peter, 2010, p.127; Hoeppner, 2013).

Hamburg attempts to reach youth through the Hamburg HipHop Academy, a city-sponsored project encouraging micro- and macro-political integration of migrant descendants through hip-hop instruction. In interviews with HipHop Academy participants, I heard stories like that of Turkish-German Yağmur Pence, who attended *Gymnasium* (college preparatory high school) in a wealthy western suburb. Her classmates told her she was not a "normal" Turk. Though as a young child she told her mother, Adile, that she felt German, others do not see her this way. Can Güleç, born to a German mother and a Turkish father, feels German and speaks little Turkish. Still, interviewees told of times when "*ethnic Germans*" complimented their fluent German. Migrant descendants, many of whom are labelled "*ethnic Muslims*" in government reports, noted how "*ethnic Germans*'" lack of awareness of cultural nuances among "*ethnic Muslims*" hinders feelings of belonging. Even migrant descendants who have fulfilled integration requirements do not escape stereotypes when acting supposedly "*normal*" (Pence, 2013; Güleç, 2013; Atalay, 2014).

Barbara Supp has shown via *Der Spiegel* that when migrant youth convey they feel unwelcome in Germany, religion becomes more appealing. When integration does not succeed, fundamentalism can become tempting and offers an outlet for discovery and self-confidence particularly for boys like Ahmed K. with lower education and employment prospects. Unfortunately, many government integration projects reach already integrated youth who are willing to attend programming (Supp, 2006). My research confirmed the vast majority of HipHop Academy participants consider themselves to be macro-politically integrated—they speak fluent German, attend *Gymnasium* or university, and some have never visited their "homeland."

What is the solution then to Germany's integration crisis? Mandatory, in-school integration programs reach students regardless of parental permission and can foster feelings of mutual understanding and cultural awareness. Still, the missing piece of macro-political integration is the bridging component, which requires "*ethnic Germans*" and migrant descendants to form interethnic relationships, be open, respect and accept rather than just tolerate cultural differences. Bridging fosters increased social capital by extending people's "radius of trust" through cooperation and mutual reciprocity (Putnam, 2000, p.22; Fukuyama, 2002, p.32-33). Eurobarometer findings show citizens and migrants believe cultural respect is key to successful integration because it promotes feelings of mutual respect (Migrant Integration, 2011, p.68-69). With mutual respect, youth can develop feelings of belonging, which catalyse a lasting connection between migrant descendants and Germany and facilitate a heightened desire to contribute to the nation-state. Nonetheless, many Turkish-German youth still feel the need to prove their "*Germanness*" and belonging. In the HipHop Academy dance theatre production *DISTORTION* by Constanza Macras, migrant descendants' monologues repeatedly exclaimed: "*ich fühle mich deutsch*" (I feel German). For macro-political integration to succeed, the youths' intended audience of German media, politicians, and citizens must accept them as equal Germans.

Chapter 8: Can Turks be Germans? - Symbolic Boundary Perception of Turkish Residents in Germany

Nils Witte

This paper[1] deals with immigrants' perceived exclusion as an aspect of their naturalization intention. It demonstrates how immigrants perceive exclusion in different ways. The analysis draws on 13 in-depth interviews with Turkish permanent residents in the German city-state of Hamburg. The interviews were conducted as part of a mixed-methods study that investigates the role of symbolic boundaries in naturalization intentions of Turkish residents in Germany. The case of Turkish residents is relevant because they constitute the largest group of resident aliens in Germany (22% of foreign pop.) (Statistisches Bundesamt, 2013a) and their naturalization rate is low compared to other third-country nationals. Their annual naturalization rate was barely 5% in the last 20 years, although the majority is eligible for German citizenship (Statistisches Bundesamt, 2013b). Finally, the requirement to renounce their former passport makes an examination of symbolic aspects of citizenship particularly interesting.

In the first phase of the mixed-methods study, Attitudes towards Citizenship and Naturalization (ACN 2012), a self-administered mail survey, was carried out reaching 249 Turkish residents of the city of Hamburg. Multivariate analysis established the significance of symbolic boundaries in naturalization decisions next to rights-oriented motives for citizenship acquisition (Witte, 2014). However, the survey leaves unanswered how immigrants come to perceive symbolic boundaries and how they deal with them. This paper is based on 13 in-depth interviews conducted in 2013 and presents initial results. It aims to improve our understanding of divergent

[1] The introduction draws on a paper that presents results from the first part of the study (Witte, 2014).

boundary perceptions and gives a first impression of how these perceptions relate to subjective meanings of citizenship.

Symbolic boundaries in the realm of ethnic groups have been conceptualized in similar ways in several studies. However, the operationalizations vary. According to Lamont and Molnár "*symbolic boundaries are conceptual distinctions made by social actors to categorize objects, people, practices, and even time and space*" (1992: 168). Zolberg and Woon understand symbolic boundaries as the outcome of a negotiation of the following questions: "*who can become a member of society, and what are the conditions for membership*?" (1999: 8). Both, hosts and immigrants take part in this negotiation. Hence, they look into public discourse and institutionalization in the realms of religion and language. Alba (2005) draws on Zolberg and Woon but further includes citizenship and ethnicity. This study is interested in immigrants' perspective on symbolic membership and the way they perceive it.

The analysis aims at tracing the processes of individual boundary perceptions from its roots to its consequences for citizenship acquisition. In this way I explore the empirical substance of the boundary concept. How do individuals come to perceive symbolic exclusion or inclusion? In what terms do they talk about it? Also, interviews provide insight into how individuals deal with experienced exclusion. The interviews are not analysed exhaustively in this paper. Some questions remain to be answered in my ongoing research. What strategies do immigrants develop to deal with exclusion and what are these strategies' consequences? How is boundary perception connected with naturalization intentions? What are potential implications of the interviews for future survey research? The interview material also provides answers to these latter questions but the respective analysis is beyond the scope of this paper. In the remainder of the paper I describe how the data was collected and analyse the interviews in order to provide initial answers to the questions just raised before I end with a discussion of results.

Data collection

Sampling

The survey allows for purposeful sampling. 109 survey respondents (44%) provided contact information and agreed to participate in personal interviews. Categories for the sampling procedure have been developed based on results from multivariate analysis. For the purpose of sampling interview participants, predictors of naturalization intentions have been condensed to two dimensions: perceived permeability of symbolic boundary (blurred vs. bright) and instrumental motivation to naturalize (weak vs. strong). Four ideal types of motivational structures result from a combination of these dimensions as shown in Table 8.1. A residual category is included for cases with neither strong nor weak motivation and/or neither strong nor weak boundary perception (R). The typology serves to organize cases and develop some guiding questions. This strategy is known as "sampling according to schedule" (*Qualitative Stichprobenpläne*) or "selective sampling" (Kluge 2010: 50ff). Interviews do not aim at gathering evidence for or against this typology but at adding new information that was impossible to obtain from survey analysis.

Table 8.1. Type construction for sampling

		Rights-oriented motivation to naturalize		
		weak		strong
Symbolic boundary perception	blurred	1		2
			R	
	bright	3		4

Since resources for in-depth interviews were limited, it was an obvious strategy to select those types that allow for the least clear predictions of the intention to naturalize. A person that perceives the symbolic boundary as blurred and has strong instrumental incentives for naturalization (2) is very likely to be inclined to acquire citizenship. In the opposite case of a perceived bright symbolic boundary and weak rights-oriented motives (3), naturalization is very unlikely. The remaining types are the most indeterminate ones. An immigrant who perceives the symbolic boundary as blurred and has a weak or no rights-oriented motivation (1), will she naturalize? And in the opposite case of a perceived bright boundary and strong instrumental motives (4), what is likely to happen? Is the rights-oriented motivation a sufficient condition for naturalization and the symbolic boundary of minor importance? Or is the perception of the symbolic boundary as blurred a necessary condition irrespective of existing rights-oriented motives? Since answers seem to be rather straightforward for types (2) and (3) and not very clear for (1) and (4), the two latter types seem more relevant for in-depth interviews. The residual category has not been considered for interview sampling. Interviews with groups (1) and (4) promise to enlighten how legal and symbolic motives are intertwined.

Interview Method

Interviews followed the approach of the Problem-Centred Interview (PCI) as described by Witzel and Reiter (2012). They were conducted in late 2013 in German with 13 participants from ACN 2012 who had consented to the follow-up. Witzel and Reiter characterize the PCI as an approach that takes the middle course between standardized non-reactive interviewing and narrative non-intervening interviewing. The main idea is to involve the interviewee into a process of active understanding. Hence, the first question is very open and ideally provokes a long opening account by the respondent. The interviewer may have several areas of interest in mind. But in the course of the interview, he follows up only on those topics that the interviewee mentions in the sequence they come up.

The opening question in my interviews refers to the nexus of immigration and integration but in a rather open way: "How was it when you first came to Germany?" Since no respondent was born in Germany, this question worked for all. Further, I addressed three additional areas of interest: experienced discrimination, feelings of accommodation, and citizenship. Besides, interviewees had answered the survey questionnaire one year earlier and therefore may have remembered a whole range of topics potentially relevant to the interviewer. Also, they knew from the contact letter for interview recruitment that citizenship acquisition was the main focus of my research. So while I did not ask them to relate to specific motives I did introduce the three areas of interest mentioned above. I introduced the issue of citizenship towards the end, in order to have them talk about their experiences first, before making them reflect on the more abstract question. Citizenship acquisition is more abstract for its effects refer to a hypothetical future. Besides, the question tends to inspire reference to the political discourse that is further removed from respondents' personal experiences.

The choice of the PCI seems adequate for the broader research design of this study. The issues involved in naturalization decisions are well researched (for Germany see e.g. Diehl and Blohm 2011, Prümm, 2004, Wunderlich, 2005); hence I started the study with a survey. Also, the research question is rather delineated. In the light of prior research, it seemed pointless to conduct fully open narrative interviews. Neither would structured interviews improve our insight from the standardized survey. The PCI allows for a rather clear demarcation of the thematic field, while leaving space for respondents' interpretations and constructions of meaning. In order to deepen insights from the survey, it seemed reasonable to introduce the two thematic fields of discrimination and accommodation in addition to the opening question and the issue of citizenship.

Interview analysis

Method of Analysis

In order to analyse the interviews in a systematic way, I organized them following a twofold strategy of "subsumptive" and "abductive" coding (Kelle and Kluge, 2010: 61) using a coding software. Subsumptive coding starts with some basic categories that are refined and changed in the process of coding by comparison among cases. Abductive codes are developed from the interviews. Initial categories were given by the interview issues: discrimination, accommodation, and motives for and against naturalization.[2] Hence

[2] The example of the initial code 'racial discrimination' may illustrate the flexibility of the coding scheme. It ended up as a sub-category to 'evaluation of Germans / Germany' and has further sub-categories of its own that specify the source or place of discrimination (e.g. 'at work', 'at school', 'police / public office' etc.).

there were some initial ideas that guided interview analysis. They followed from both theory and empirical findings. The interviews aim at understanding how individuals relate to their country of residence and what considerations they make when thinking about citizenship acquisition. Some will mention these 'boundaries' as consequential for their naturalization intentions, others will not. As reported above, there have been various ideas of how to measure symbolic boundaries. While some scholars refer to institutions and public discourses, this study is interested in immigrants' perspective on symbolic membership and their perception of boundaries. Hence, codes are introduced only for boundary aspects mentioned by respondents. Similarly, there are no prior assumptions about individual conceptions of legal membership. In this way, the interview analysis was open to new findings and respondents' interpretations of their relation to the majority group.

Boundaries Between

Most respondents perceive symbolic boundaries between immigrants and the majority group as bright. However, they have different reasons for doing so and different ways to cope with it. Interviewees' experience of boundaries can be roughly differentiated into two thematic fields: ethnicity and religion. The separation into two fields is an induction from the interviews that is ideal typical and does not translate back to the empirical level in all cases.

Ethnicity

The ethnic component of symbolic boundary construction pools three markers mentioned in the interviews: language, phenotype and name. Several interviewees believe naturalization would not change their standing with respect to the majority group the reason being their ethnicity. In their experience, having an accent, dark skin, black hair, or a Turkish name, inhibit their recognition as German fellow citizens. In other words, the visibility and audibility of their ethnic difference represents a symbolic boundary. This section contrasts the boundary perceptions of Yakup Karadeniz and Ali Bilgic[3]. The comparison is meaningful because they immigrated under similar circumstances, but diverge in their experiences with the host country.

[3] All interviewee names are pseudonyms.

They both immigrated in the framework of their apprenticeship, to learn their profession in a German hotel but diverged in their careers.

Yakup Karadeniz' professional life has been rather successful but he is frustrated with German society. Experiences of racial discrimination mix with other experiences of rejection: His children face problems in the labour market because of their ethnicity and religion, he reports personal experiences of racism with police officers or other public officials, and finally, the 'NSU affair' augmented his mistrust.[4] These experiences have created a general discomfort.

German society doesn't perceive foreigners the way they are as human beings. Instead they focus on the passport, if you have citizenship. That's very annoying. That is why I don't want to become German, because - to what end? I can work, I earn my money, I pay taxes and I have been in Germany for 42 years. For 42 years! And I cannot vote. Why not? (Yakup Karadeniz)

This discomfort keeps him from naturalization in spite of his interest in franchise. Obviously, he could naturalize, if voting rights were his main priority. However, he would lose one club membership without full recognition in the other club.[5] In other words, bright boundary perception impedes naturalization.

I won't change citizenship because of that. Why? I'll always remain Turk. My identity card holds my name. I am Yakup Karadeniz, hence, I remain Yakup Karadeniz. No matter if the ID cards says ,German'. How can I be German? I have a different name. (Yakup Karadeniz)

Although Ali Bilgic's professional life was less successful than in the case of Yakup Karadeniz, he is more optimistic about the relation to the majority group. Interestingly, he mentions his phenotype as a reason for the absence of recognition issues. So, he does perceive an

---

[4] The NSU-affair refers to a series of xenophobic murders committed by a small group of neo-Nazis (**N**ational **S**ocialist **U**nderground) during the 2000s uncovered in 2011. It gained wide media attention for racially biased police work and the still unclarified involvement of liaison officers.

[5] According to Turkish law, he would not lose all rights connected to Turkish citizenship (Law No. 5901/2009 Turkish Citizenship Law, Art. 28). But many Turkish residents are either unaware or mistrust the administrative implementation of that law.

ethnic boundary, but does not feel excluded by it because people ascribe to him a non-Turkish ethnicity.

Well, as I said, I never really had any problems in Hamburg I'd say, because I always looked white. I will show you some pictures later. People always thought I was Italian or Greek, I wouldn't know the difference between Greeks and Turks, they look alike. (Ali Bilgic)

This may seem like blurred boundary perception that alleviates the intended citizenship acquisition. On closer inspection, however, boundary perception can be said to have more than one dimension. One dimension refers to boundary perception and another one captures if it applies to the interviewee. Also, different boundaries seem to apply to different immigrant groups. Ali Bilgic perceives a bright boundary towards Turks, but the one that applies to him and other "Italians or Greeks" is blurred. This seems to be a way to cope with exclusion in an optimistic way. Along those lines, Ali Bilgic reports an experience of racial discrimination on the job market that might have led other immigrants to perceive a bright boundary. He was refused on the telephone on racial grounds when he applied for a job, but succeeded when he introduced himself personally the following day. Ali Bilgic expresses understanding for his later boss's initial racial prejudice and frames the episode as a personal success. As the other interviews show, this is only one of several responses to experiences of exclusion. Similar experiences lead to different symbolic boundary perceptions. A systematic analysis of responses and eventual typecasting will be part of my ongoing research.

Religion

Several interviewees mention discrimination on religious grounds as harmful to their relation with the majority group. This section contrasts Hatice Yilmaz with Enes Demir for their opposing experience with religious discrimination. In total, six respondents mentioned their religiosity. Three respondents explicitly identified themselves as Muslims and in three cases it was mentioned in passing. In three cases respondents mentioned their wife's or children's religiosity, and in one case the children showed me handicrafts they made in the mosque. That leaves three out of ten respondents who did not hint to their religiosity in any way.

Hatice Yilmaz is the interviewee with the strongest experiences of exclusion. She says to have lived a wonderful childhood in Germany. Discrimination started when she entered the labour market. Her experiences are mostly personal and she has a general feeling of exclusion as in the case of Yakup Karadeniz. In her experience being Muslim and being foreign are intertwined; difference to Germans is generally understood as a deficit. However, among the outsiders she feels particularly rejected. She attributes that to her headscarf in combination with her confidence and achievement.

Since I am covered, since I am Turkish, and since, well, I have to say it strikes me that Turkish women, or especially Muslim women, those who are covered – those who are open [without veil], they are well received and so on – but if you are covered and you made it somehow, it always strikes me, it's not well received, they don't want that. (Hatice Yilmaz)

The experience of discrimination against covered women is echoed by several male interviewees who talk about their female family members. They know of discrimination on the street and on the labour market. For example, Yakup Karadeniz' daughter was dismissed two times from her job as a hairdresser after she started wearing a headscarf. Hatice Yilmaz' experiences of religious discrimination are intertwined with ethnic discrimination. During the interview she repeatedly refers to a "we" that she contrasts with "the Germans". On probe she specifies this category as including those who are branded as Turkish or "foreigner".[6] Also, she suggests that some persons are not recognized as Germans after they acquired German citizenship.

If you are not like a German, with respect to faith, with respect to going-out, and this and that, then you are labelled as Turk, foreigner, that's that. And we always means: We, who are labelled as foreigner, no matter if you have German citizenship or not. (Hatice Yilmaz)

[6] Legal meaning and common understanding of the term *Ausländer* (foreigner) diverge. In everyday understanding it may refer to persons who are Germans but have non-German ancestors. Some interviewees used the term in a neutral way as a self-description. However, the term often has a negative connotation and is common in xenophobic contexts.

As the following passage shows, Hatice Yilmaz does not cope as easily with the experience of exclusion as Ali Bilgic. Her experiences of discrimination have been more frequent than Ali Bilgic's and she has not found an optimistic interpretation.

For me this country is not our country but it is not different either, at least I don't perceive it different. On the contrary I would eventually behave differently in my country, because I would simply feel at home. Here, I am more careful, more respect of course, that is even stronger for me then. Because, we may live here, we may do everything just as everybody else. That is why I appreciate this country. But unfortunately I have to say, they don't appreciate that in us. And that's what makes you sad [...] It's really, if you understand everything, then everything hurts you, when they talk to you, when they swear at you, when you are subject to discrimination, then you don't feel really comfortable here I have to say. (Hatice Yilmaz)

Enes Demir is a practising Muslim like Hatice Yilmaz but does not experience his religion as problematic in relation to the majority group. The relevance of religion in his life is underlined by his choice of the mosque as the interview venue. During his personal guided tour through the mosque he mentions that the municipality sponsored their heating system, which may support a feeling of recognition. Also, his employer's approval of his breaks for prayer seems to be a relevant ingredient to his accommodation. While his boundary perception is similar to that reported by Hatice Yilmaz, he does not experience it as problematic; he does not feel rejected. Enes Demir has no intention of acquiring German citizenship, but the bright boundary apparently is not the main obstacle. There simply is no sufficient incentive for citizenship acquisition.

Well, I am foreigner, but I haven't felt like a foreigner often. [...] We cannot adapt appropriately here in Germany, neither in Turkey, we are foreigners everywhere. And we got to live like that, won't change. I repeat, even if I have German citizenship, I am foreigner, I will remain foreigner, hence, nothing will change. I don't object German citizenship, but I don't need it. [...] (Enes Demir)

Interviewer: And could you tell me how you feel in this country?

Very well. I like living in Germany. I feel good, really. Also, I can practice my religion here. (Enes Demir)

Enes Demir's reaction to the perceived exclusion from the majority group is still different from those described above. While his boundary perception is similar to Hatice Yilmaz', the way he deals with it is more optimistic. In his perspective, the boundary between Turks and Germans is a social fact that is beyond his control. While this might upset other persons, he apparently is not concerned.

Discussion

This paper provides answers to the first of the three sets of questions introduced above. How do immigrants come to perceive symbolic boundaries and in what terms do they talk about them? One aspect of their symbolic exclusion is the visibility and audibility of their 'Turkishness'. Namely, dark skin, black hair, foreign accent, Turkish name, and headscarf are perceived as irreconcilable with being German. Experiences of discrimination are another reason for experienced exclusion and bright boundary perception. These findings support and supplement past research on symbolic membership in the German context. Anthropologists and Sociologists have looked into the negotiation of boundaries from both sides. Miller-Idriss (2006: 558ff) found similar experiences of symbolic exclusion among naturalized children of immigrants. They describe how their self-definition as German is questioned by other Germans for reasons of phenotypical otherness. The headscarf of Muslim women has been an issue in public debates time and again but increasingly so after 9/11. According to Amir-Moazami (2007) the headscarf is not only object of debate; for Muslim women it may also help to define their identity as distinct from the German one. A further parallel to my findings in her study of second generation Muslim women is their continued self-definition as foreigners after naturalization. However, the construction of non-German identity (as Turkish, Muslim, or foreign) goes hand in hand with an appraisal of liberal values of German society and the inclination to live in Germany for good (ibd.: 228f.). Other research shows Germans' boundary definitions. Birth in Germany, being of German descent and fluency in German seem to be basic criteria for recognition as German by other Germans (Mäs et al 2005; Schneider 2002). Similarly, Mandel (2008) describes the active discursive exclusion of Turkish immigrants and their descendants from what is defined as German by the mainstream. In my study, most respondents perceive Turkish and German identities as non-transformable natural givens. The interviews cannot answer, though, to what extent boundary making by both groups supports this perception. However, many respondents report having experienced discrimination or they know of it via their family members; those are instances of boundary making by Germans. However, immigrants deal with those experiences in different ways. In my ongoing research I want to analyse their responses systematically. Second, I will describe respondents' conceptualizations of citizenship to disentangle the relation of symbolic boundaries, legal incentives and citizenship acquisition. Third, the in-depth interviews being part of a mixed methods study, I want to explore potential implications for future survey research.

While most research on naturalization behaviour compares immigrant groups, this study focused on one country of origin and one host country. In this way it was assured, that immigrants' perceptions of the host country would not depend on different legal statuses and different legal requirements for citizenship acquisition. Their different perceptions can be attributed to their experiences with the majority group and the way they deal with those experiences. This paper shows in which terms Turkish residents perceive exclusion. Finally, it reminds us that citizenship acquisition not only a legal but also a symbolic act. When legal incentives are absent, naturalization becomes a merely symbolic confirmation of membership in a society. In the past decades, Germany has successively reduced the legal requirements for citizenship acquisition. The state is now aware that immigrants will stay for good but will contribute to political legitimacy only once they are citizens. However, full membership in both legal and symbolic terms will be achieved only once people accept that today Zuhal and Yakup can be German. As this paper shows, such recognition would be an invitation for immigrants to become members of the polity.

Acknowledgements

I want to thank participants of the Migration Working Group at the European University Insitute (21 May 2014) and Turkish

Migration Conference 2014 at Regent's University London (31 May 2014); and Fran Meissner and Jan Dobbernack for comments on earlier versions. Also, I want to express my gratitude to Matthias Wingens and Herwig Reiter for helpful discussions of the initial interview guideline.

Chapter 9: The Second Generation's Discovery of Transnational Politics via Social Media

Necdet Coşkun Aldemir

The term "transnational politics" first began to emerge in the literature in the early 1970s with a focus on the changing patterns in the world politics and strategic linkages between states and non-state actors (see: Rosenau, 1969; Kaiser, 1971). Even in these early diagnoses, it was presupposed that there had been a growing -cultural, financial and political- interaction between diverse actors in the societies of different nation-states. Without a doubt, within the contemporary global processes that call into question the sovereignty of the nation-states, which are conceptualized as "denationalization" (Sassen, 1996; 2003) or "postnational" model (Soysal, 1994), transnational politics is much more influential in today's global political conjuncture and its importance is increasingly growing. The changing conditions of current global politics empower the positions of NGOs, interest groups and non-state actors and signify the emergence of new players in the global political arena. Within this context, migrants' transnational political practices gain particular significance and not only do they now more directly affect the way in which home countries' policy-making processes are shaped, but they also have a considerable impact on the positionalities of the countries of residence and on the global public opinion at large.

On the other hand, one of the most important elements that have contributed to and made possible this current condition of global politics is digital technologies and their implications for societal domains. Digital technologies introduce new spaces in which migrant population can take part in transnational political activities in different ways. Although it is quite early to suggest that these kinds of practices that migrants engage in on digital platforms have a considerable impact on their transnational political activities, it can be suggested that these newly emerging spaces of resistance, action and representation deserve an analysis of their own. The present study tries to examine the possible consequences of digital technologies for the second generation's participation in transnational political activities within the framework of the changing patterns of collective action.

Method

The method of the study is mainly based on the basic principles of the multi-sited ethnographic approach (Marcus, 1995). It should be acknowledged, however, that one of the most important deficiencies of the empirical side of the study is that the author was not in Gezi Park during the occupation. On the other hand, the author took part in nearly all the demonstrations that were held to support the Gezi Park protests in Izmir, Turkey from 3 June 2013 to 28 August 2013, and had participated three times in the protests which were related to the Gezi Park process in Frankfurt am Main, and one time in Cologne, Germany. Moreover, one Turkish migrant political organization that was one of the main organizers and supporters of the Gezi Park protests in Germany had been regularly visited for nearly four months. Furthermore, social media had been actively used in order to observe, follow and participate in the online side of the protests since the Gezi Park process began.

Additionally, during the anniversary of Gezi Park, followed by a sixteen-day fieldwork in Istanbul, the researcher had engaged in local forums, solidarity groups, squatted houses and demonstrations, and had the chance to observe closely how digital technologies are embedded in the processes of "the making of" a transboundary –if not transnational- movement that is strictly local.

Finally, in the last part of the paper, the analysis of a Facebook page on which a demonstration was organized and held in Germany in order to support Gezi Park protesters in Turkey is presented. A piece of the selected "naturally occurring data" (Silverman, 2001) obtained from this Facebook page were analysed. The main method of the analysis used is conversation analysis, more specifically Sacksian membership categorization analysis.

Migrants and Transnational Politics

Migrants' transnational activities have caught particular scholarly attention since the 1990s (Levitt & Jaworsky, 2007). The general consensus reached on this issue was the realization that migrants actively and simultaneously developed, maintained and reinforced various kinds of ties with the countries of origin and of settlement. It was argued that with these sustained ties between at least two different societies, migrants created "transnational social fields" (Basch et al., 1994; Levitt & Schiller, 2004) or "transnational social spaces" (Pries, 1999; Faist, 2000) in which they live by crossing the borders of two countries and deriving a new culture from the two. In an initial attempt to describe this new condition of migrant population and to suggest an analytical framework for migration research Glick Schiller et al. (1992) offered the term "transnationalism" and named this new migrant type as "transmigrants." According to them, the old concepts that describe migrants as passive, uprooted and subaltern subjects should be abandoned. On the contrary, this new kind of migrant population actively builds their ties (cultural, familial, religious, political etc.) between the two countries and strategically positions themselves in accordance with the various situations they encounter. By doing so, they experience new and constantly changing patterns of life in which they try to find new ways to survive and construct new identities.

Migrants' transnational political activities reflect maybe one of the most intricate webs of interconnectedness within their complicated transnational life-worlds. As Østergaard-Nielsen (2003a, p. 760) states: "*The field of migrants' transnational political practices is as complex as the multilevel processes, structures, and actors involved.*" Thus, in order to facilitate the understanding of migrants' transnational political activities, it would be useful to follow Itzigsohn et al. (1999) and differentiate two analytical concepts regarding these activities. According to them, the conceptualization of transnational fields should be detailed. Pursuing Mahler's (1998) suggestion, they argue that the transnational practices of migrants might be defined and structured by using the scale of "narrow" and "broad" as the two different poles of migrants' transnational activities. Accordingly, narrow political transnationalism involves institutionalized and regular (mostly via political parties or organizations) political activity, while broad political transnationalism denotes occasional, personal and irregular involvement in political activities.

This distinction between the intensity of transnational activities facilitates the understanding of migrants' transnational political practices by shedding light on the other and poorly-studied dimensions of transnational politics. It has been well documented[1] that migrant organisations and well-institutionalized brunches of home country associations and political parties play a significant role in transnational politics; and that the network of migrant political organizations and political party branches in the countries of residence is so efficient to such an extent that it might mobilize a huge amount of people, particularly when an important political event occurs in the home country. On the other hand, looking at the issue of migrants' transnational political practices from an institutional perspective makes it difficult to see the other aspects of the issue and over-simplifies the real complexity of the phenomenon. First of all, the institutional approach is itself deeply problematical. As Landolt (2008) points out, the institutional approach views migrants as passive subjects within the vertical institutional relations and presupposes an isolated organization that does not have any relations with the other civil society actors within its environment. In this way, it inevitably fails to capture the intricate network of interactions within migrants' transnational political paths. Moreover, the representative quality of migrant organizations is also in question: "*The main problem with such an approach is that the organizations are not necessarily representative of the communities as a whole.*" (Østergaard-Nielsen, 2003b, p. 11) Furthermore, as Østergaard-Nielsen (2003a) observed, migrants who are members of political parties or migrant organizations are much fewer in quantity compared to those who are not active in any political organization. Although there are very limited studies on the second generation's participation, some of the existing studies also reflect a considerable amount of doubt about the role of conventional organizational mobilization and social capital

[1] See for a detailed case study of Turkish and Kurdish migrants' transnational political practices in Germany: Østergaard-Nielsen, 2003b. See also for a comparative study of Turkish migrant organizations: Ögelman, 2005.

(Togeby, 2004) and the taken-for-granted patterns of political participation for the second generation (Mügge, 2010).

Therefore, there is little doubt to suggest that the issue of migrants' broad transnational political practices is an increasingly important subject of inquiry within the wide area of transnational politics. On the other hand, digital technologies create new spaces for political activism, particularly for occasional, non-institutional and sporadic forms of political activism.

Digital Technologies and New Actors

The contentions about the possible reflections or consequences of digital technologies (and social media[2] as a part of them) for societal domains have led to an ongoing and highly contested discussion in social science. Some researchers[3] have eagerly highlighted the democratizing and participatory nature of the new digital technologies. On the other hand, others[4] seem to view these technologies with suspicion and suggest that there are hardly any new things that can be found in digital technologies. In the same vein, the debate on the role of social media in collective action seems to consist of the two sides. Some researchers argue that social media is the main determinant of recent social movements and has the ability to trigger them. As Graziano (2012, p. 539) has noted: "*The growing role of the social Web has been regarded as the real driving force behind the riots: that is to say, the virtual Agora was the first place where it was possible to (re) negotiate legitimate claims for democracy; it was only in the second stage that crowds took to the streets.*" Other researchers' contentions are, however, that social media does not cause any collective action, but rather it makes it easier to spark social movements rapidly. "*Social media should be seen as facilitators of protests rather than causes.*" (Wolfsfeld et al., 2013, p. 120)

In these debates, it might be fair to follow Sassen's (2006) suggestion that while approaching this issue, not only should it be

---

[2] I would like to thank Heike Greschke for her critical comments on the analytical value of the concept of social media and advising me to take a more critical stance on the possible consequences of digital technologies for societal domains.

[3] See chiefly: Castells, 2008; Mitra & Watts, 2002; Nisbet et al., 2012.

[4] See for an extensive critic of ICTs' discourse: Robins & Webster, 1999; see also: Lunt & Livingstone, 2013.

avoided focusing merely on the technological aspects of digital technologies, seeing them as "all-powerful" devices and disregarding the social environments where they are used, but treating them as if they bring nothing new and that they can be substituted for old technological formations should be also avoided. According to Sassen, the Internet has created a new kind of activism and politics that enables small-scale, local and resource-poor organizations, groups or individuals to participate in cross-border politics. In this way, they can become actors who take part in a global network without being restricted to the limitations of their local environment but at the same time continue playing their local roles (in work, family, community etc.). As Sassen (2006, p. 338) has put it: "*This produces a specific kind of activism one centered on multiple localities yet connected digitally at scales larger than the local, often reaching a global scale.*" She also argues that this kind of political activism occurs in the shapes of two different types of digital activism: the first type is the place-based mostly in cities[5] activists who struggle for local issues in offline settings by seeking political subjectivity in global networks; the second type is only active online and their struggles do not usually cause actual collective action.

These two types of digital activism should be elaborated in order to uncover the new possibilities digital technologies provide. The first type is based on the local struggles, which are completely mediatized by nearly all kind of digital technologies (tablets, smart phones, laptops, video recorders, digital cameras etc.). It can be seen in recent social movements (Occupy Wallstreet protests, Indignados, Arab Spring, 2009 Iranian presidential election, Gezi Park etc.) that digital technologies have played a significant role in nearly every stage of these instances of collective action. Particularly, social media and more specifically social networking sites are widely used not only for organizing, but also for exchanging information, communicating, discussing, acting (as hacking attacks), and sharing[6]. These digital

[5] The importance of cities for transnational grassroots migrant activism was first realized by Smith (1994) who termed this "transnational grassroots politics." Of course, much earlier Lefebvre (1996) had already discovered the importance of cities for collective action. See also for a recent work: (Harvey, 2012).

[6] Of course, this is not to suggest that social media causes social movements. It is only a

platforms that are publicly and globally accessible allow for participation in the online side of the movement from all around the world on conditions that there is an internet connection and make it possible to interact instantly within global networks. All of these recent movements, moreover, are strictly local (and/or multi-local); so that camps, squares, barricades or spatial struggles mark them in an apparent way. This fact calls for an explanation of how thoroughly local movements (or struggles) are able to spread quickly across the globe and become visible on a global scale, and even very individual attempts can mobilize a considerable number of people, most of whom are not politically active in an institutionalized political organization.

Latham and Sassen's (2005) concept of "sociodigitization" is a very significant analytical attempt which has been made in order to illuminate this issue. The term sociodigitization connotes a process in which many aspects of social and political life have been undergoing a fundamental transformation into digital forms (texts, images, codes etc.). Once an existence is digitalized, it gains the quality of "hypermobility" that enables it to circulate through global networks instantaneously. They suggest three dimensions of sociodigitization: "*In some cases sociodigitization is 'derivative' –a mere instrumentality of these dynamics- but in others it is 'transformative' –by reshaping social relations- and even 'constitutive' –by producing new social domains of action.*" (Latham & Sassen, 2005, p. 3) They argue that what is being transformed in this process is not only information, but also the "logic of social organization, interaction and space." According to them, society and technology should not be thought of as two different entities. In many respects, they are nested in one another: while technology reshapes society, socio-cultural conditions also determine the use of technology. This mutual interplay between technology and society comes into being in the

useful tool (for now) for the movements and the history of social movements is full of the instances of using appropriate devices creatively and opportunistically for their struggle. What makes social media (and social networking sites in particular) so important for recent social movements is, I believe, that it creates a media effect by providing a relatively free, publicly accessible and well-known (within the infinite depth of the Web) platform in which individuals and groups can share and create content, communicate and interact with each other, and represent themselves.

reciprocal embeddedness of digital and non-digital processes, and consequently, redefines the conventional meanings of the local and of the global. As Sassen puts it:

"*For example, much of what we might still experiences as the "local" (an office building, a house, or an institution in our neighbourhood or downtown) is something I would rather think of as a microenvironment with global span insofar as it is deeply inter-networked. Such a microenvironment is in many senses a localized entity, but it is also part of global digital networks, which give it immediate far-flung span.*" (Sassen, 2006, p. 346)

The most crucial contribution of this analysis is that it enables us to grasp concurrently the spatial quality of a locality and its new dimension when it connects to the global networks. Contrary to the other interpretations of the effects of digital technologies, which disregard the importance of space and celebrate the inauguration of a new digital age in which much of what can be thought is possible, this analysis acknowledges the gravity of space[7] and turns its main focus toward the impact of digital technologies on the spatial entity that is highly digitalized and immersed in networked practices. Digitalization and networked practices, of course, produce new (electronic) spaces. However, it is neither the technological capabilities nor the infinite possibilities of global networks that qualify these new spaces. Rather it is the networked interaction among people on digital platforms which produces and forms these kinds of spaces. This formulation recapitulates the analysis: "*space is organized; organization is spatial and interactive; interaction requires organization; and interaction produces spaces.*" (Latham & Sassen, 2005, p. 10)

In many respects, during the occupation, Gezi Park (and also the other localities when the protests spread and became multi-local) was a kind of locality where every inch of it was deeply inter-networked by the pervasive use of the digital technologies that connected it with global networks.

---

[7] Henri Lefebvre's (1991) seminal work offers the most comprehensive and meticulous theory on space.

Gezi Park: Building a Local Movement within Global Networks

On the 27th May 2013 at around 23:30 the destruction of Gezi Park began. The first tweet that announced the destruction and called for immediate action was sent on the same day at 23:47. After the call, approximately 20 people gathered in the park at night and managed to stop the destruction (Özyer, 2014, p. 19). When they decided to keep guard over the park and build their tents there, nobody could expect that this would be the beginning of one of the most massive series of uprisings in the history of modern Turkey.

Gezi Park is a small urban park in the very centre of Istanbul. It takes place next to Taksim Square and Istiklal Street which is the most central area of the city. The government declared that Gezi Park was going to be destroyed and replaced with a shopping mall as part of the ongoing urban renewal projects. The spark of the uprisings was the anecdote above. The excessive police violence against peaceful activists in the following days increased the number of protesters who had mostly organized via social media. Uncompromising attitude of the government, growingly continued police violence and an obvious self-censorship situation in the mainstream media in Turkey caused an unprecedented degree of public anger and civil disobedience and turned this relatively small-scale environmentalist local struggle into countrywide and multi-local anti-government protests beginning from 31st of May 2013. Until the eviction of Gezi Park on the 15th June, the movement had already become a global phenomenon with a large amount of global public attention and support[8].

It can be said that from the very beginning to the very end, digital technologies were at the heart of the Gezi Park protests. This was mostly because the mainstream media in Turkey ignored the protests and even when they turned into massive uprisings and spread across nearly all the big cities, they were still pretending that nothing important was happening in the country. This fact inevitably rendered social media the main source of information. Particularly Twitter,

[8] There is no doubt that it can (and should) be said a lot of things on Gezi Park protests. See for some interpretations of the protests in English: Kuyumlu, 2013; Örs, 2014; Žižek, 2013; Catterall, 2013; Göle, 2013. There is also a comprehensive online book: http://yasarkenyazilantarih.com/historyrecordedlive/ available on: 26.07.2014.

Facebook and YouTube[9] were the most influential sites by which information was shared. Due to this extraordinary self-censorship (Genç, 2013) situation in the mainstream media, protesters used all the available channels through which they could make their voice heard and tried to inform people about what was going on. They created various publicly accessible user accounts on social networking sites, a lot of blogs on which they regularly posted information about Gezi Park, a radio station that broadcasted in different languages, a TV channel that broadcasted live on the Internet, they also advertised an announcement in New York Times and Washington Post by collecting money on a website called "*Indiegogo*," to name just a few.

Moreover, during clashes with the police, protesters actively used social media in order to organize themselves and navigate among the places they ran off or went to help others. Especially Twitter was extremely effective, since it can be applicable to nearly all kinds of digital technologies (computers, laptops, tablets, smart phones, etc.) and also due to its feature of "*retweet*" that can transmit a piece of information to a massive population by circulating it among the individual networks. This was the case to such an extent that one of the protesters could find his lost bag in one of the other districts of the city; or that they could identify the licence plate of a car which had driven towards the protesters and injured them; or that they could ascertain a police officer's official number written on his helmet.

A group of researchers collected data, which consists of tweets that had been sent during the protests. It was stated in this report[10] that "*What is unique about this particular case is how Twitter is being used to spread information about the demonstrations from the ground. Unlike some other recent uprisings, about 90% of all geolocated tweets are coming from within Turkey, and 50% from within Istanbul.*" Furthermore, a high percentage of tweets sent in Istanbul were coming from the places around Gezi Park and Taksim.[11]

---

[9] It should be noted that social media should not be thought as independent websites. On the contrary, the various links that are shared on these well-known platforms might navigate users to other websites.

[10] This report received from: http://smapp.nyu.edu/reports/turkey_data_report.pdf available on: 27.07.2014.

In other words, the places where there were violent clashes between the police and the protesters. The active use of social media in the middle of the protests might be an explicit indicator of the imbrication between digital and non-digital processes in this instance of collective action.

The role of social media in the process of Gezi Park was definitely far beyond only information sharing or organizing. Within this process, these digital platforms underwent a radical transformation as well –in terms of getting politicized of these domains of social life- and became an intrinsic part of the movement. That is to say that the users who had not been interested in political issues before were increasingly getting politicized on social media platforms. The online survey (Bilgiç & Kafkaslı, 2013) which was conducted between 3th and 4th June 2013 with more than 3,000 participants indicates that 75.8% of the respondents had actively participated in the protests on the streets; and that 53.7% of all the participants had never taken part in a political demonstration before. This survey also underlines the fact that the majority of the protesters were young people by stating that 63.6% of the respondents were between 19 and 30 years old.

These distinctive features of Gezi Park, namely that it was a civil youth movement which was marked by the political use of personalized digital communication technologies, render it a unique example for the examination of the potential impacts of digital technologies on the second generation's transnational political engagements.

Social Media and the Second Generation in Support of Gezi Park in Germany

In migration studies, the issue of migrant generations is quite vague. There are not any definite and explicit categories over which researchers have reached a compromise. Within these debates, Fouron and Glick-Schiller (2002) propose expanding the concept of the second generation including all the children of immigrants regardless

[11] See for a visualization of the tweets that had been sent from Istanbul between 31 May 2013 and 3 June 2013: http://www.youtube.com/watch?v=oXW3WVeMC64 available on: 28.07.2014.

of their place of born or place of residence. They argue that these young people all live in one transnational social field because of their parents' enduring transnational connections and actively and simultaneously take part in the "personal and political events" in both of two countries. For Fouron and Glick-Schiller, the transnational field in which migrants live produces a different kind of nationalism, what they term "long distance nationalism."[12] This "ideology of belonging," according to them, is not only an imaginary commitment or belief, but it might also appear in the forms of direct action and participation in the political events of the homeland.

Most of the demonstrations that took place in Germany to support the Gezi Park protesters in Turkey might be seen as an obvious reflection of this long distance nationalism. A considerable number of the Turkish migrants living in Europe (and also in the US and in Australia) have been actively supported the Gezi Park protests in Turkey since the beginning of the protests. Among these countries, Germany stood out due to its high percentage of Turkish migrant population. Consequently, it was held simultaneous demonstrations that were organized mostly via social media and initiated by ordinary individuals[13] nearly all the major cities in Germany, especially during the first two weeks of the Gezi Park process.

One of these demonstrations was taken as an example and analysed below. For the sake of anonymity, the names of people were changed in the data extract. Changed names were written in boldface and additional information was provided by using square brackets ([]).

This demonstration was organized as a Facebook event and initiated by a university student. It took place one of the big cities in Germany. The event had been created on a publicly accessible Facebook page one day before the demonstration was carried out. After creating the event, organizer sent invitations to all his friends

---

[12] The term "long-distance nationalism" was first coined by Benedict Anderson (1992) who argues that current phase of capitalism creates a new type of nationalism.

[13] Of course, there were also many demonstrations that were mobilised by organizational support. However, even in these instances social media was used to mobilise people or to announce the demonstrations by a large majority of political organizations, especially by resource-poor ones.

living in the city demonstration would be held. His friends also sent invitations to their friends and some of them tried to make the event visible by sharing the event on other digital platforms like Twitter, etc. On the same day, another person who was organizing another demonstration as a Facebook event in the same city offered to combine the two demonstrations. Even after the combination of the two events, organizers expected that 150-200 people would participate in the demonstration. Until the demonstration began, however, the numbers in the event were as follows, "2,403 going, 297 maybe, 16,602 invited."

On the page of the event, participants discussed almost every stage of the demonstration. While some of them were suggesting possible slogans that might be chanted, others were uploading the photos of the placards they had prepared. The topics discussed on the page were various, ranging from legal procedures for staging the demonstration to the preparation and translation of the press release. Most of the posts on the page expressed solidarity and a high percentage of them included visual media content (videos, photos, the links of live streaming videos etc.) regarding the Gezi Park protests in Turkey. During and after the demonstration, participants uploaded the videos and photos that they took in the demonstration to the page as well. The data extract below were taken from this page (accessed on: 18.11.2014) and consists of the comments that had made to a post criticizing some chanted slogans during the demonstration.

1	**T.B.C.:** Insanlari suclamamali. Hayatlarinda ilk.. Organize edenler gucsuz kaldi. Onunla alakaliydi tamamen.. 01.06.2013, 10:56	**T.B.C.:** People should not be blamed. This was the first time in their life.. It was the organizers who were incapable. This was completely related to this.. 01.06.2013, 10:56
2	**F.E.:** cunku benim gibi bir suru kisi irkci sloganlari duyup terketti alani. 01.06.2013, 12:18	**F.E.:** because a lot of people like me left the place after they had heard racist slogans. 01.06.2013, 12:18
3	**T.F.U.:** Arkadaşlar bazı	**T.F.U.:** Dear friends of course

	sloganlardan biz de hoşnut değildik tabi. Dediğiniz doğru, tecrübeli değildik, olduğumuzu da hiçbir zaman iddia etmedik. Tamamen spontane bir sivil girişimdi bu. Anlamsız şeyler yaşandığı oldu. Ama konunun özünden sapilmadi bence. Yine de gelen destek olan herkese teşekkürler. 01.06.2013, 12:56	we did not like some slogans too. You are right, we were not experienced, we have never suggested that we are experienced as well. This was completely a spontaneous civil attempt. Meaningless things also happened. But I think that the essence of the matter was not strayed. After all thank everyone who came and supported. 01.06.2013, 12:56
4	**T.B.C.:** Kürt arkadaşları aralardan gördüm , ancak tgblileri susturamadım. Megafon aradım ama o ara polis yolu açın merdivenleri boşaltın demekle (sanırım **T.F.U**'dı) sorumlu arkadaşı oyalıyordu. Ne olursa olsun ordaydık.. bir dahakine tecrübeliyiz. Ayrıca **T.F.U**'a verdigi emek icin tesekkür ederim. 01.06.2013, 13:21	**T.B.C.:** I saw some Kurdish friends , however I could not silence supporters of the tgb [*TGB* is a political organization]. I looked for the megaphone but meanwhile the police was busy with the person in charge (I think it was **T.F.U**) by saying open the way evict stairways. After all we were there.. next time we are experienced. Moreover I thank **T.F.U** for the effort he made. 01.06.2013, 13:21

In the first line, T.B.C's first sentence introduces the category "guilty." Identifying the category, we can see some *category bound activities* (CBAs) in her line, such as "to be blamed" and "to be incapable" and, at the same time, we can also recognize the *members* "those who are guilty" and "those who are innocent." In her second sentence, it can be obviously seen that people (in this context Participants) are described as innocent because of their inexperience. Her third sentence "It was the organizers who were incapable." not only directly addresses the member guilty ones (Organizers), but also builds a *standardized relational pair* (SRP) between the members, Participants/Organizers. According to Sacks, by invoking SRPs, a set of moral and mutual rights and obligations is constituted. Giving this base, it might be suggested that T.B.C. is speaking within a *membership categorization device* (MCD), "organization." That is to say that she perceives this Facebook event as any other protests organized by any ordinary political organization. In this way, she ascribes some certain responsibilities, tasks, and duties to the organizers, such as determining the slogans that will be chanted, or preventing some groups of people chanting some slogans that might be offensive to the others. These membership categories (Organizers/Participants) are also what Sacks (1995: 249) calls *positioned-categories*. For him, some pairs of categories might be higher or lower in relation to one another (like Teacher/Student, Adult/Child, Employer/Employee etc.) and these positioned-categories can be used for *prising* or *degrading* the Members. In this sense, it can be said that T.B.C degrades the organizers by describing them as "incapable."

F.E., on the other hand, introduces a new "two-set class" under the category of Participants by saying that "a lot of people like me." Taking the Indexicality (Garfinkel, 1967) of the conversation into consideration, we can describe this new two-set class as Turkish Participants/Kurdish Participants. In this way, F.E. also sets up a new MCD, "ethnicity."

In the third line, one of the organizers, T.F.U., tries to explain the situation. With his first sentence, he indicates that he was not one of those who had chanted racist slogans. In his second sentence, he benefits from the clear correlation, which was built by T.B.C. in the first line, between the category "innocent" and the description "being inexperienced." Moreover, his sentence "This was completely a spontaneous civil attempt." is a *modifier* for the MCD "organization" that was set up by T.B.C.. By stating this sentence, he implies that he is an organizer but the things that can be expected from a formal organizer should not be expected from him. And by virtue of the use of this modifier, as Sacks (1995, p. 45) underlines, "*in the last analysis he's like the others.*" Accordingly, it can be clearly seen from his last three sentences that he does not seem to speak as a person who organized a political demonstration any more, but rather he speaks like a person who arranged a social event (like a get-together, a party, a meeting, etc.).

In the fourth line, T.B.C. says "some Kurdish friends" instead of saying "some Kurdish people/persons" The word "friends" here invokes some SRPs, such as mutual support, care, help, solidarity etc. By using this word and invoking these SRPs, she implies that she could not be those who had chanted some racist slogans. We can also see here that she recalls the MCD "ethnicity" that was set up by F.E.. Here it can be recognized that within the sequence of conversation, the production of the category guilty, which first T.B.C had directly attributed it to the Organizers, has shifted. The last part of her first sentence reveals the new member that has been categorized as guilty, namely supporters of the political organization TGB. In this way, she introduces a new two-pair class under the category of Turkish Participants: Civil Turkish Participants/Partisan Turkish Participants. Furthermore, within the context of the demonstration, the verbs like "to silence" and "to look for" are some CBAs that usually identify the member Organizers. This might allow us to suggest that the modifier T.F.U. had used works well, and that now T.B.C. perceives T.F.U. not as a formal organizer, but rather as a demonstrator like the others who is as responsible as (and not more responsible than) anyone. The consecutive use of the subject "We" in her last sentences also signifies the same membership category. The sentence "next time we are experienced" shows that the correlation she built in the first line (inexperience=innocent) is still in use. Her last sentence, on the other hand, constitutes a new reciprocal positioning and, consequently, replaces the procedure for *degrading* with the procedure for *praising*.

The analysis of the data extract is showing us that on this digital platform not only do they manage to discuss, arrange, mediate, organize and eventually hold the demonstration, but there they can also overcome the difficulties they might encounter in all stages of the event. Even after the demonstration is held, the communicative process[14], which had first begun online and mostly based on textual forms enriched by visual images and then transferred to the offline setting with face-to-face encounter with the participants, is still continuing. In this data extract, moreover, it can be also seen, what

[14] See for an extensive and meticulous analysis of computer-mediated sociality and of the complex communicative processes of community building and developing a sense of togetherness online: Greschke, 2012.

ethnomethodologists would call, how social order is achieved. The process of the reconstruction of social order, in the data extract, reveals the significant differences between this sort of political mobilization and the conventional forms of collective action. The former seems to be a combination of computer-mediated sociality and political activism; what might be called "computer-mediated political action."

Conclusion

It is well-documented that media[15] has always been one of the main catalysers of the processes of transnational politics between the two countries. On the other hand, the possibilities presented by digital technologies provide new channels through which migrants can engage in transnational political activities in different ways. During the Gezi Park protests, it became clear that these new channels could be highly effective, particularly for the second generation's mobilization. Giving the analysis of the data extract, it is fair to say that with its computer-mediated[16] nature, social media adds a new dimension to the forms of migrants' transnational political activities in a deeply and thoroughly mediatized way.

[15] Since the very beginning of the Turkish labour migration to Germany, media (media for migrants, in the case of Open Channels [Offene Kanäle] media "to" migrants, and also ethnic migrant media) has always been closely linked to politics. See: Kosnick, 2000; 2007a; 2007b.

[16] See for an extensive and meticulous analysis of computer-mediated sociality: Greschke, 2012.

Chapter 10: Political integration of the German-Turkish youth in Berlin

Mine Karakuş

The main aim in writing this paper on German-Turks is to present an exploratory analysis on the Turkish community in Germany. Through a series of in-depth interviews with younger generations of German-Turks in Berlin, it is focused on their preferences concerning citizenship issues and attitudes towards their home as well as host countries. The role of their overall approach towards citizenship issues in shaping their political participation strategies in both German and Turkish contexts is also underlined.

The main question revolves around the issue of citizenship preferences of the German-Turks. I explore the simple question about the extent to which their citizenship preferences and attitudes towards citizenship at large facilitate their political integration in Germany. I accordingly ask whether or not and to what degree the German-Turks are politically integrated into German society.

In accordance with the main question, the argument were developed under two main issues. The first issue concerns the German Citizenship tradition and how this tradition shapes citizenship preferences of the German-Turks. The second main debate revolves around the analysis of political integration and political strategies of the German-Turks. Since it is the citizenship that determines the conditions under which subjects become members of the political community, I present the political participation strategies that were shaped within the framework of German policies.

Literature review

This section will analyse what has been discussed in the literature on Turkish immigration to Germany under two main titles; the process of Turkish immigration and Turkish community formation in Germany, development of German policies towards non-Germans and the situation of contemporary Turkish community in terms of naturalization preferences and political strategies.

The Process of Turkish Immigration to Germany

The period after World War II was that of high industrialization and rapid development in the North and West European countries, which exacerbated the structural difference between the North and South European economies. This polarization between the North and South also shaped the route of the migratory flows from the less developed south to more developed capital expansion in the North. Within this context, emigration in the 1960s was considered as the major cure for the foreign currency and unemployment problems in Turkey, by both sending the unemployed and also getting their remittances as foreign currency. As for the Federal Republic of Germany, the already existing labour shortage was exacerbated by the construction of the Berlin Wall in 1961. Consequently, a bilateral agreement was signed in 1961 between Turkey and the Federal Republic of Germany, which set the terms of recruitment. According to the agreement, the requests were made by the German Federal Labor Office and its representative bureau in Istanbul to the Turkish Institute of Labor. In the 1960s, thousands of emigrants from Turkey in surge of higher wages were destined towards Germany. To illustrate, in less than a decade, the number of Turks in Germany increased to around 469.200 by 1970 (Gitmez, 1983: 19). When discussing the initial status of the Turkish immigrants as guest-workers, Kadioglu (1997) used the term *Konjonkturpuffer* for describing the role of Turkish immigrants as "*shock absorbers regulating the ups and downs of the economy*". In that sense, the Turkish community in Germany started to develop in 1960s with intense labour recruitment. Their status within the society as the welcomed konjonkturpuffer has started to change towards unwanted 'Muslim intruders' (Kadıoglu, 1997: 84). The 1970s was marked by a severe energy crisis and global economic problems that exacerbated unemployment in European countries and elsewhere. As a precautionary measure for the mounting problems, German authorities decided to stop labour recruitment.

While stopping the potential incoming labour, social rights of the immigrant workers were recognized. Rights to retirement and other social security provisions such as healthcare, unemployment benefits, and child benefits coupled with the ongoing political and social unrest at the home country gave the Turkish immigrants an incentive to stay and bring their families. Therefore, in 1970s immigration from Turkey was in the form of family unification.

Empirical Discussions

After providing the historical process of Turkish immigration, the discussions in the literature that are relevant to the main issues of this paper will be scrutinized.

Citizenship Preferences

Explanations for how citizenship preferences of the German-Turks have been discussed in the literature were provided in Diehl and Blohm's (2003) article entitled, Rights or Identity? The article questions the main motive for Turkish immigrants to naturalize that they gain more rights and benefits. Diehl and Blohm (2003) hypothesized that,

"...Turkish migrants are more willing to 'change flags' because naturalization offers a means of transferring formal allegiance to a group with higher social status, especially for those who have achieved a high level of individual assimilation." (Diehl and Blohm, 2003: 134-135).

Their findings reveal that the benefits of citizenship have no significance on the naturalization preferences of the Turkish immigrants. On the other hand, it is the upward mobility and belonging to a more prestigious group that underlies the naturalization preferences of the assimilated immigrants. They argue that it is more likely for an assimilated person to become a citizen. Furthermore, Diehl and Blohm (2003) see the only significant advantage of the legal rights that citizenship brings as participating in the elections. Diehl and Blohm's survey conclude a similar argument that it is more likely for a person to naturalize, who is interested with politics.

However, the data presented by Kaya and Kentel (2005) hardly supports Diehl and Blohms's argument. Despite the fact that a considerable number of the participants stated their positive attitudes towards German citizenship, there is a prevalent disinterest among the

German-Turks about German politics. Parallel to Diehl and Blohm, formal political participation through voting may facilitate the German-Turks to be more familiar with German politics and those individuals interested in German politics may choose German citizenship out of political concerns. However, as will be discussed further, it turns out that in line with Kaya and Kentel's (2005) findings, political participation in its orthodox sense does not have an importance in participants' citizenship preferences.

Political Strategies of the German-Turks

Ostergaard-Nielsen begins her discussion by defining two forms of political activities as Immigrant Politics and Homeland Politics. According to Ostergaard-Nielsen, homeland politics, which was prevalent for the Turkish immigrants until the late 1970s and early 80s, "*denotes migrants' and refugees' political activities pertaining to the domestic or foreign policy of the homeland*" (Ostergaard-Nielsen, 2003b:21). Immigrant politics are the political activities that migrants or refugees undertake to further their situation in the receiving country, such as obtaining more political social and economic rights or fighting discrimination, which characterizes the political activities of immigrants after the 1980s (Ostergaard-Nielsen, 2003b: 21). Thirdly diaspora politic is as a subset of homeland politics confined to those groups that are barred from direct participation in the political system of their homeland. By presenting this categorization, she mainly argues that, migrant politics and homeland politics cannot be discussed separately for "*immigrant political claims for religious and ethnic distinctiveness send strong (...) signals (...) to the political regime of the country of origin*" (Ostergaard-Nielsen, 2003b: 21). In discussing the process of ethnicization of Turkish political participation strategies in Germany, Kaya (2000) states the German policies towards immigration as the main reason for adoption of a particular participation strategy. He divides the participation strategies of the Turkish immigrants into three groups as immigrant, minority and diasporic strategies. The first two are ethnically based strategies as the outcome of Guest-worker ideology and the assimilationist ideologies of Germany, while the third one is culturally based due to the implication of multi-culturalist policies (Kaya, 2000:43). What

Kaya (2000) argues about this particular issue is how the assimilationist and exclusionist policies of the conservative government that came into power in 1982 has shaped ethnically based political mobilization of the Turkish immigrants towards the host land.

Kaya (2000) also refers to multiculturalism as a factor for ethnicisation and culturalization of Turkish immigrant strategies. He argues that, the immigrants conforms the standards shaped by the majority as multiculturalism, confined to their cultural and religious identities (Kaya, 2000: 58). He criticizes multiculturalist policies with regard to Turkish minorities in the sense that cultural representations become more important than defending their political and economic interests (Kaya, 2000: 99-107).[1]

Citizenship

Citizenship is a contested concept and it is not attempted to get on a difficult task of analysing the whole dimensions of its nature and development. It is assumed that the German-Turks perceive and experience the inherent inequalities of the German notion of citizenship, which affects their preference over German citizenship. Thus, while developing the discussion on the link between the respondents' preference over German citizenship and its role in their political integration, the inherent inequalities of the notion of citizenship will also be examined. For this purpose, I will refer to Thomas Humphrey Marshall's essay entitled Citizenship and Social Class' that was published in 1950 from his lectures in Cambridge University. His overall discussion over the British citizenship practices and social class is based on the assumption that citizenship as an equality in status perpetuates social class divisions as an inequality in wealth. Marshall admits that, the citizenship rights that were supposed to bring equality are discriminatory in effect (Marshall, 1950: 114) While surveying the role of social services, for

[1] Kaya argues that multiculturalism reinforces the power relations between the host culture and the minority culture. Minority and immigrant cultures then started to be realized as exotic entities, which are tolerated and protected by the hegemonic culture. Additionally by referring to Foucault he also adds that, through giving a sense of freedom in the cultural sphere, the hegemonic political powers make the immigrants and minorities governable.

achieving a certain degree of equalization, Marshall mentions that even though some sort of equality in income is established between *the 'more and less fortunate'*, the quality issue of the given service is quite problematic (Marshall, 1950:114). Furthermore, the citizenship rights and services reinforce the structural differences based on socio-economic levels within a given society (Marshall, 1950: 112). Segregation of lower classes starts from schooling, the procedure of getting the state benefits remain as the symbolic ways to remind the individuals who are entitled to social remittances, their not so 'bright' status within the society. In the case of German citizenship, existence of similar inequalities will be demonstrated, but in contrast to the Marshallian approach, the focus will be on the ethnic basis rather than on the social class.

In a broad definition, citizenship has two main aspects; membership to a given community and designated rights and obligations for those who belong to that community.[2]

Marshall's notion of citizenship is active participation of full members of a community. In a sense, within a society the nature of class structure and the discourses on citizenship such as equality are inconsistent with each other. The class structure is inherently unequal and perpetuates the economic social inequalities in a society whereas, citizenship as mentioned before gives equal rights to all citizens. However economically disadvantaged classes have access to poor quality services that citizenship ensure and/or even face symbolic limitations and barriers due to their class position. This constitutes the inconsistency between the nature of class structure as inequalities and the discourses on citizenship as providing all citizens equal rights and services. The practicability of rights of citizenship according to Marshall is highly questionable because of the existing class system. Halfmann (1997) refers to the issue of an individual's relation with the state by differentiating between political inclusion and state-mediated inclusion. With this definition, citizenship is not a matter of membership but a matter of membership to different systems. Resident non-citizens are members of labour markets that are highly

[2] For Dell'olio (2005), citizenship as a legal concept is based on community and set of rules that misses the sociological aspect of the concept' wherein identity plays an important role'.

regulated by welfare provisions. Thus states through taxation, social benefits and compulsory schooling, include resident non-citizens within the welfare system. But members of a nation defined as an imagined community based on a common identity, are entitled to both social protection and political participation. Therefore membership to a community does not necessarily involve citizenship but defines the limits of it.

As for the acquisition of citizenship, there are two different legal principles, jus soli and jus sanguinis. In the former one, citizenship is based on birth in the territory of the country and involves incorporation into various groups. Jus sanguinis is the ethnic model, which is based on descent of a nation. As in the case of the Federal Republic of Germany, an imagined community based on common descent is constructed and the citizenship is given only to those who are considered members of the imagined collective identity. In Sassen's (1999) terms, German conception of nation as *jus sanguinis*, regards a nation as if it were a 'biological inheritance rather than a cultural acquisition'. By demonstrating the development of German notion of citizenship, I will draw attention to the impact of citizenship on ethno-cultural based inequalities.

The reason for discussing German citizenship tradition in detail is to understand the underlying reasons for the particular rhetoric and strategy that German-Turks employ in approaching their problems. This is because the deeply rooted tradition of jus *sangunis,* as well as the denial of being a country of immigration has resulted in the exclusion and marginalization of the already settled non-German populations.

In the postwar era the non-German populations grew with the economic boom and labour shortages, as the ethno-national definition of German citizenship became more salient. From 1970s onwards, unemployment and economic recessions were presented as an excuse for restrictive policies towards immigrants. However, it was against the non-German population that the politicians problematized German economy. To put everything in a nutshell, what accounts for the restrictive policies is the famous refrain that Germany is ‘kein Einwanderungsland' [not a country of immigration]. The reasoning underlying the refrain as 'Germany is not a country of immigration for non-Germans' makes the naturalization policies insufficient to deal with the already settled non-German population. Hence the denial of being a country of immigration has been the motto for three decades summarizing the reasoning behind the naturalization and citizenship policies of Germany.

The Citizenship Law that came into force in January 2000 was an important turning point for Germany. Its importance lies in the fact that, with this legislation the long established assumption that Germany is not a country of immigration was officially denied. In replacing its tradition of blood principle with acquisition of citizenship through birth, Germany officially accepted that it is a country of immigration. Therefore the 2000 Citizenship Law is revolutionary in the sense that, it constitutes admission of Germany to being a country of immigration.

Generally speaking, to become a citizen, a foreigner needs to fulfil the following conditions; legal residence in Germany at least for 8 years, to have a residence permit, to accept the Basic Law, not to engage in any activities infringing the Constitution, to have sufficient skill on German language, not to depend on social security and unemployment benefits and finally an individual should not have any criminal records. (Web site German Consulate of Istanbul article 4(3).)

Previously, the children of Turkish immigrant parents who in many cases were born and raised in Germany, speak German perfectly as their native tongue, but were not considered citizens until the citizenship law was accepted. But with the new legislation, a child born to foreign parents can become a citizen under the conditions that one of the parents have been legally residing in the country at least for eight years or have permanent residence permit at least for three years. Therefore, the 2000 Citizenship Law signifies a departure from the deeply rooted tradition of jus sanguinis, by giving citizenship to children born to non-German parents. The German tradition of citizenship was primarily based on the principle of jus sanguinis, which has gone through a remarkable transformation. Such citizenship policies in a multicultural, multi-ethnic society imply exclusion and political marginalization of a considerable population. Acknowledging the shortcomings of excluding and stigmatizing certain groups within the society as foreigners was an important step taken back from the deep rooted ethnically based understandings.

Methodology

My intention in this section is to lay down the basic procedures and experiences I had in conducting the two main branches of my research. My original intention was to interview 30 people between the ages 17 to 30; 15 women 15 men from different socio-economic backgrounds but the sample constituted 22 individuals 11 men and 11 women

Interviews were composed of two parts; the first one was in-depth interviews with long intervals and open-ended questions. These questions had four sections concerning individual experiences of being member of a minority group and to what culture and society he or she feels closer to. The questions about citizenship and political participation are asked to understand what they attribute to being a German Citizen, giving up Turkish Citizenship or being a dual citizen. In other words, from these interviews I was expecting to clarify the linkage between citizenship, political participation and social integration.

Entering the field was the most time consuming and problematic part of my research. Rather than directly contacting my sample group, I tried to establish links through organizations and foundations. Making direct contacts would be less time consuming but also it would have been harder to convince people to talk about some personal and sensitive issues. The second problem encountered was to ask the interviewees to allocate their two hours' time for interviews. A third issue that the interviewees regarded as a problem was the language. In order to reach the sample of young people, contacts were made with Turkish and German organizations in Berlin.

German-Turkish youth in Berlin

This section will focus on my observations and interviews during fieldwork in Berlin. As mentioned in the introduction, the arguments presented center on the main question of how the level of political integration of the German-Turks and how their citizenship preferences facilitate political integration. The section on citizenship preferences of the German-Turks analyses the importance of German citizenship for the participants. As will be discussed further, the only reason that German-Turks prefer German citizenship is their utilitarian concerns. It will be assumed that their emphasis on the practical rather than political reasons highly stems from the experiences of discrimination based on their citizenship status in their daily affairs.

Political Strategies

This section analyses the strategies that the participants employ in political participation. Political participation indicates how the participants raise their demands, whereby the overall discussion will be centered on ethnicization and culturalization of German-Turks' political participation strategies.[3]

Coming to the political strategies of the German-Turks and the participants in particular; general indifference with the political issues, voting for the same party without showing any interest in that party's objectives[4] and making politics through ethno-cultural and

[3] It may be useful to remember Kaya's (2000) and Ostergaard-Nielsen's formulations. Kaya (2002) divides the political strategies of the German-Turks into three parts and Ostergaard-Nielsen into two by taking diaspora politics as a subset of homeland politics. Leaving aside the conceptual differences, they both refer to the same three phases: politically passive guest workers who only follow the political developments at home, until the late 1970s. The second phase is the continuation of the home political divisions in the host country and political orientations were directed towards Germany rather than homeland politics. The assimilationist pressures triggered by the right wing governments on the Turkish immigrants prompted them to seek their rights and interests under their own ethnic or religious communities. The communities defend their interests and struggle for their rights separately and demand distinctive recognition both at home and host country. Therefore the 1980s witness an increasing proliferation among immigrants from Turkey based on their ethnic and sectarian origins. In the third phase as a diasporic community the German-Turks' increasingly used naturalization by shifting interests from Turkish to German politics, with an increasing need to defend their rights and interests in Germany and at the same time seeking special recognition in Turkey that resulted in the emergence of a diasporic political strategy. Tw different points comprise the issue; first the voting patterns and the underlying reasoning in their voting preferences will be discussed. Secondly, the apolitical methods of the German-Turks, as participants' lack of preference of German citizenship out of political reasons and have no concern about joining the elections reveals their apolitical methods of participating in German politics that will be further elaborated.

[4] In discussing the voting patterns and preferences, no matter what their world views are, the entire participants vote for SPD (Social Democratic Party). The participants were highly divergent in terms of their ideological orientations from one spectrum of conservative and Islamist to another more liberal dimension. However such political orientations are not reflected in their voting preferences as all the participants with one exception stated that they vote for SPD. Social Democrats with their more liberal and pluralist politics, are also highly supported by German-Turks, no matter how diverging their norms and values may be. The

religious references are all aspects of the German-Turks' political strategy. Structural exclusion from the German political system as denizens[5], the only way for the German-Turks to voice their demands and complaints was through their own ethnic and religious organizations.

This exclusion from the German political context is also reflected in their rhetoric. To give empirical evidence for their ethnic based strategy of political participation, I will refer to how the participants discuss the most important problem in Germany as unemployment. As mentioned, political participation is the way that the subjects raises their concerns and demands.

Relatively, when stating their concerns about such a mounting problem as unemployment, participants refer to their ethnic backgrounds, blaming the German employers for discrimination or the politicians and the society for presenting the Turkish community as responsible for unemployment. In that sense, the participants do not politicize the issue of unemployment with reference to state policies, globalization, or capitalism. Rather they prefer ethnic connotations in their discussion on unemployment. Therefore the participants reflect their ethnic based political strategy with their rhetoric in discussing the problems.

A second example of how their political strategies are reflected in their discussion refers to Mesut. He problematizes his experience of encountering certain questions from Germans about Islamic practices, for instance, *"why the Muslims don't eat pork, I know Turkish Muslims drink raki why don't you drink, why do women cover their head, you treat women like a slave, these rules aren't mentioned in Koran right?"* (From the interview with Mesut). Mesut continues by complaining "*Germans have already accepted the gay people. But our existence is too much for them.*" Mesut's criticisms of German society and his demands for acceptance with his Islamic identity are the

---

ethnically based political strategy of the German-Turks is reflected in their voting preferences. Their situation as being ethnic and a cultural minority community and the fact that the Social Democrats have closer policy objectives to minority groups than other parties make the SDP as the party representing the German Turks within the German politics.

[5] Denizens are described as immigrants with permanent residence status including social and civil rights. The denizen category includes the citizenship of the non-EU states who reside and enjoy the rights with the citizens except the political rights (Faist, 2001:46)

implications of the ethno-cultural and religious means for political strategies. Kaya (2000) explains the above mentioned case by stating that the process of culturalization reduces the problems of social discrimination, exclusion and racialization in the society to the level of cultural and religious differences(Kaya, 2000: 97-99). Mesut's statements present evidence on the implications of political exclusion and multi-culturalist policies as the participant essentializes religion and culture in making politics. Kaya (2000) mentions that freedom to cultural and religious expression became important for the Turkish people in Germany. As a result of the multi-culturalist policies, the cultural struggle rather than political struggle is emphasized for the German-Turks in protecting their interests. According to Ostergaard-Nielsen, diaspora politics are the "*subset of homeland politics confine to those groups who are barred from direct participation in the political system of their homeland.*" (Ostergaard-Nielsen, 2003a:21). She differentiates diaspora from immigrant politics: in the former the political participation is through ethnic and cultural mobilization of the diaspora oriented towards homeland politics. Latter one protects their interests and voices their demands in the hostland. She discusses how immigrant and homeland politics are inseparable in party-political, religious and ethnic mobilization of the Turkish and Kurdish communities.

Both Cemile and Osman criticized a local parliamentary of Turkish origin who argued that covered women should take off their headscarves in order to better integrate. Cemile, Mesut, and Osman mentioned these disputes on headscarf and integration as *"they -some politicians of Turkish origin- come out with silly ideas, she says take of your headscarf Why the headscarf why? The German newspapers make fun of it -look the Turkish immigrants are fighting among themselves."* (From the interviews with Cemile, Mesut and Osman)[6]

[6] "I have a certain culture, I cannot leave it, they say take your headscarf off. Why don't you respect my opinions?"[Ben belli bir kultiirden gelmisim bi günden bi güne bırakamam ki bazi şeyleri adamlar şey diyo iste başörtünüzü bırakın benim düşüncelerime saygı niye göstermiyosun] Osman, "A woman Parlimanterian insisted on that if Turks' do not cover their head they would be better integrated. They are doing silly things, why the headscarf, why?"[Turkler eger basortii takmazsa daha çabuk entegrasyon olabilirmis diye bi söz çıkardı kadın milletvekili, Türk Sacma sapan şeyler çıkarıyorlar ortaya, niye yani niye başörtü] Cemile.

This particular case is quite relevant to what Ostergaard-Nielsen mentions as the inability to separate homeland and immigrant politics. The participants transmit the same political issue centered on the headscarf to a much different platform of German immigrant integration politics. The political debates on headscarf revolve around the Muslim population in Germany of predominantly Turkish origin. What the headscarf symbolizes in the German context is a failure of integration, fundamentalist tendencies of the Turkish immigrants, and, in general, the incompatibility of Islamic Turkish culture with the German cultural and social system that is quite different from the political debates on that particular issue in Turkey. Therefore the headscarf issue is not a political debate that is essentially German, but introduced by the religious practices of the Muslim immigrants of predominantly Turkish origin.

A second reason for mentioning the headscarf issue is to give further evidence that, in line with Kaya's (2000) argument, the political mobilization of the German-Turks is within the cultural and religious sphere. What the participants infer from political participation is the struggle for their cultural and religious rights. Consequently, the essentialization of culture, ethnicity, and politics making through rhetoric marginal to German political tradition entail that the participants are not totally integrated to the German political community. However such a conclusion should not imply that their marginalization is being problematized and the blame is put on German-Turks for being marginal. On the contrary, it is the German legislative framework that leads to the formations of the ethno-cultural communities that are marginal within German politics and the German policies towards the ethnic minorities that resulted in the spread of marginal essentialist rhetoric among the German-Turks.

German or Turkish citizenship

In this section, the citizenship preferences of the participants and the extent to which the preferences affect their political integration will be analysed. The main argument on the findings is that, the participants choose to become German citizens for practical reasons. The importance of political participation and political integration through voting rights is minor among the perceived advantages of

German citizenship. Scrutinizing the citizenship preferences indicates that German citizenship is instrumental for the political integration of the German-Turks by granting the membership to the political community.

Within the legislative framework of German Citizenship Law, the important distinction between a citizen and a resident non-citizen is their political participation. In other words, non-citizen German-Turks, can enjoy the same social and civil rights that a German would. In this sense, it is expected that the most important motivation to become a German citizen would be the right to vote and to be elected. When the advantages of being a German citizen are asked, all the participants emphasize the same point; less paper work and formalities, enabling mobility and higher chances for employment. Escaping long procedures and formalities in everyday issues become salient in the preference of German citizenship.

From Kaya and Kentel's (2005) research, a general view on the issue of citizenship and political integration can be grasped. Accordingly, there is a strong tendency among the German-Turks for naturalization; 59% of the participants state that they are either German citizens or applicants for naturalization. However the same research also reveals the fact that 60% of the participants are indifferent to German politics. (Kaya and Kentel, 2005: 79-80). Kaya and Kentel's data support my findings that preference for German citizenship does not accompany willingness for membership to the political community.

Accordingly, naturalization does not entail political integration and indifference with politics in general, but seems to be independent of citizenship status. It is also important to avoid reducing political participation to the orthodoxy of voting and petition. If political participation is defined as subjects' raising demands and protecting interests then participation can be in any form. However exclusionist policies until the 90s marginalized the Turkish population within German politics; the Turkish immigrants sought their rights and protected their interests through their own religious and ethnic networks, which were outside of the German political context. Furthermore, the multi-culturalist policies confined ethnic minority policy making to the cultural sphere. Hence, due to this peculiarity of the German system, citizenship as defining membership to the German political community is important in the way for people to resolve their problems.

While discussing the impact of German citizenship on integration to the political community, the fact should be underlined that, naturalization cannot be regarded as an important parameter for the integration of German-Turks. On the contrary, non-citizen respondents in the interviews are well integrated to the German society in terms of participating in social life, education, language, and employment. For instance among the non-citizens, Osman sees Berlin as his home country rather than Turkey.[7] Similarly all of the non-citizens plan to continue their life in Berlin rather than moving to their parents' home country. Therefore, citizenship should not be taken as a mark of the level of integration. During in- depth interviews, in almost all cases, it was strongly emphasised that "no matter if you are born here, you have lived here all your life, if you don't have a German passport, and you face long procedures for a simplest thing like renting a DVD."[8]

For instance Ferhat, Gorkem and Hilal;

"If you want to rent a film, you need to get a card from the rental store. And for that they say, you need to bring this paper that paper, birth paper. For carrying I don't carry a book with me now." (Interview with Gorkem)

"If you register somewhere it i done right away. If you have a Turkish passport it lasts very long, you need a paper from the police, they want to see some other papers. In German citizenship all is written." (Interview with Hilal)

"For the most simple thing like library registration, you bring bunches of paper. Now passport is enough, you get rid of the paper work." (Interview with Ferhat)

Obviously, not being a member of the German political community through citizenship make the German-Turks suspects in

---

[7] "I call myself Berliner because I was born here and raised here, I see this city as my own country, I know everywhere..." [Tabii ki bu benimseme olayi benimsemeyle ilgili mesela ben Berlinliyim diyorum. Çünkü ben burda dogdum büyüdüğüm icin ben bu sehri sanki benim memleketi gibi goruyorum heryeri elim gibi biliyorum simdi...] Osman.

[8] It was the first response from all of the participants to the question "what is the advantage of becoming a German Citizen?"

the eyes of the German authorities. According to Ferhat; "*as if yo will take the film and run away to Turkey. They treat you as such so I am more comfortable with the German passport*"

What has been revealed from the participants' reasoning for their preferences of German citizenship is their experiences of inequalities and their perceived discriminations related to everyday issues. Therefore it turns out to be that the reasons for the participants to prefer German citizenship are practical; having a German passport does not infer self-identification with Germaneness for the diasporic German-Turks. Similarly, being a non-citizen also does not imply detachment from the German society. In that sense, carrying the status of citizenship is not a determinant factor in the identity formation of the diasporic self. Furthermore, being a non-citizen also does not interfere with the participation of the diasporic self to the social, economic and to some extent political life in the society. Accordingly, it seems that German citizenship facilitates political participation of the German-Turks, while it can also be suggested that due to the meanings that the German-Turks attach to German citizenship, its role in their political participation is not as significant as expected.

Conclusion

The research presented in the preceding sections was aimed at unfolding two main points. One concerns an exploratory depiction of the citizenship preferences of the German-Turks. Another is concerned with preferences of the German-Turks that facilitate their political strategies.

Mainly, the way the German-Turks perceive their citizenship has important implications for the way they resolve their own problems in Germany. As examining the issues, three important points unfold; conceptual definitions and the development of the notion of citizenship; empirical significance in comparison to the previous findings; and policy conclusions on how German-Turks develop and express their strategies as the means through which they resolve their problems. Within the above mentioned framework, the findings can be summarized under two main categories. The first concerns the notion of German citizenship and its implications for the way that the

German-Turks perceive their own citizenship status. Secondly the role of their citizenship perceptions has an impact on the way they voice and resolve their community concerns.

To begin with German-Turks' citizenship perceptions follow the German understanding of citizenship. In several cases, it was mentioned that the deeply rooted tradition of *ius sanguinis,* which defines German citizenship over ethnicity has important implications for exclusion of the German-Turks. As a result of the long lasting exclusion from the German political community, the German-Turks were inclined towards their own ethnic and religious enclaves for political claims making. With this regard, the research reveals the fact that apoliticisation of the German-Turks as a result of the German understanding of citizenship is manifested in the way that the German-Turks perceive their citizenship status For instance participants focused on the importance of German citizenship as membership to the German political community. Therefore as a result of the peculiarity of the German notion of citizenship, the Turkish community channelled towards other mechanisms that can be considered marginal to the German context- for political participation.

In examining the factors, it was found that the participants are more familiar with Turkish than the German rhetoric, regardless of their level of social integration. Explaining the political issue within the Turkish perspective despite their education and following up the German media implies that, the German-Turks' political language is primarily oriented around Turkey, hence not politically well integrated to Germany.

As for policy conclusions, it was assumed in the introduction that the way German-Turks perceive their own citizenship has important implications for the way they resolve their own questions. In that case, if political strategies are taken as the way the individuals resolve their problems and raise their demands, then it can be suggested that; emphasizing German citizenship on utilitarian grounds, internalizing the status of foreignness, facilitate the German-Turks' rhetoric and approach towards the political issues. To put everything in a nutshell, the findings of the research refer to the main question from two different points: how the participants perceive German citizenship and how their perceptions are related to their political strategies. I conclude that, the German-Turks' perceptions about their citizenship status; identification with their ethnic origins rather than their German citizenship, and only emphasizing the practical importance of carrying the German passport have implications for the way the German-Turks voice their problems.

Chapter 11: The role of Turkish community organisations in Berlin: Their role in Turkey-Germany and Turkey-European Union relations

Selcen Öner

For a long time, German citizenship policies made it almost impossible for Turkish immigrants to naturalize and become part of the political community. This lack of formal opportunities led immigrants to develop a more civil society-orientated means of participation (Odmalm, 2009: 154). During the early to mid-1960s, they avoided organized political activity. But as temporary guest-worker programmes led to settlement, Turkish immigrants started to express diverse political identities and engage in group activities. The internal divisions over goals and strategies weakened Turkish community's potential (Ögelman, 2003: 166-167). By the 1980s, the Turkish network of organizations had become the broadest of all immigrant groups in Germany, although it was more polarized along political lines than any other ethnic group (Schoeneberg, 1985: 424).

Turkish immigrants have established several civil society organisations (CSO) s in Germany. According to Sezgin (2011: 237-243) they usually mobilize around homeland political agendas and express their thoughts about Turkish foreign policy. Many of them transfer remittances to Turkey. Access and cohesion are crucial factors in understanding the influence of the immigrant community on policy making at the national level. Immigrants have the potential to influence their host country's policies, including its foreign policy. However, this potential can only be realized if the immigrant community is large enough, has access to political power and speaks with a single voice (Ögelman *et al.*, 2002: 162). In Germany, Turkish community organizations have defended their rights vis-à-vis German political parties and local and the federal German state authorities. As a result, Germany's institutions have gradually begun to take these organizations seriously and consider them as representative and consultative bodies in immigrant issues (Yurdakul, 2006: 436).

Immigrant organizations in Germany have not been given any special role in the formulation of integration policy, and formal links with organizations are not well established. Although few provisions exist for the collective participation of immigrants at a federal level, there are crucial differences at the local level, depending on the local government's orientation towards these organizations. Moreover, there is a high degree of variance in terms of funding for immigrant organizations, which again often relates to the attitude of the local government (Odmalm, 2009: 154-155). As Kaya and Kentel (2005: 10) argue, in response to Germany's exclusionary *auslander* status attitude towards Turkish immigrants, the latter have tended to develop strong ethnic structures. In addition, the lack of political participation and low level of representation in Germany has made them direct their political activity towards Turkey, which has also received encouragement from Turkey in the form of networks of consular services and other official religious, cultural and educational organisations. Ostergaard-Nielsen (2000: 23-38) argues that the way in which Turks organize has not only depended on Germany's institutions, but is also related to Turkish immigrants' socioeconomic position, developments in Turkey, and developments in Turkey-EU relations.

The German public and its politicians have mostly viewed Turkey's EU membership bid through the lens of Turkish immigrants' experience (Humphrey, 2009: 142). Turkish immigrant organisations are transnational, thus, they may act as a 'bridge' between Turkey and Germany, and regarding Turkey-EU relations. However, they have many limitations to be influential in this realm.

This article first explains the role of Turkish community organisations in Berlin, their relations with German and Turkish civil society, with German political parties, and lastly their perceptions about Turkey's EU membership bid and their role in Turkey-EU relations are evaluated. During September 2012, the author conducted semi-structured in-depth expert interviews with the representatives of several Turkish immigrant organisations in Berlin, having various ideological characteristics and dealing with different socio-economic issues related to Turkish community. Because of the time constraint, interview cannot be conducted with the representatives of Alevi

Community Organisations, Kurdish organisations and some Islamist organisations in Berlin. Other interviews were conducted with Rupert Strachwitz, a specialist on civil society in Berlin, and with Faruk Şen, who is the head of TAVAK[1] (The Foundation of Turkey Germany Education and Scientific Researches) in Istanbul.

The Role of Turkish Community Organisations in Berlin

Turkish immigrants have established several CSOs in Germany focusing on cultural, political and social issues. In particular, assistance organizations, hometown associations, women, student, parent organizations and professional organizations, such as workers, businessmen and teachers associations have also been established (Sezgin, 2011: 237). According to Şen (2012), Turkish community organisations in Germany include five main types: religious organisations, political associations, fellow citizens associations and professional associations, sports clubs and business associations. The largest are religious organisations. For Şen, the most influential ones are *Milli Görüş* (National Thought) and Alevi Community Germany. There is a serious competition among religious organisations, and also among business organisations. However, they are rarely able to act together when there are events that affect whole Turkish community in Germany, such as extreme-right violence against Turks in Möln and Solingen. According to Şen (2012), even though the Turkish community has a 50-year background and it is the biggest community in Germany, its influence has been only gradually increasing because they came as immigrant working class. Yılmaz (2012), the head of the Union of Craftsmen and Artisans of Berlin (TUH) and Akarsu Association, criticized very low level of participation of Turkish community in social and political life. He stated that 'because of low educational level, social and political fragmentation of the Turkish community, its participation level and influence in social and political life in Germany is still low. However, the situation is gradually improving.'

More multicultural cities like Berlin and Hamburg have created favourable settings for funding associations, and they have also

[1] This foundation was established in 2008 in İstanbul by 28 Turkish and German people to improve Turkey-Germany relations.

established links between immigrant organisations, governmental bodies and political actors. Yurdakul (2009: 155) argues that increasingly open attitudes of Berlin's political elite have led to close relations with certain Turkish community organizations, especially in the area of integration.

Turkish immigrants arrived in Berlin relatively late compared to the rest of Germany, firstly between 1964 and 1968. Berlin's Turkish religious organizations are usually ignored as partners by local authorities, generally not receiving financial support or having official contact with politicians. Instead, Berlin's politicians tend to rely on contacts with left-wing Turkish community organisations to gain access to the community, which has made these organisations more influential than those representing other ideologies (Vermeulen and Berger, 2011: 162-174).

Turkischer Bund in Berlin-Brandenburg (TBB) and the *Türkische Gemeindezu Berlin* (TGB - *Cemaat*) are two of Berlin's umbrella community organisations, with established ties to German state institutions and political parties. Each claims to represent Turkish community in Berlin, while appealing to two different political tendencies: the social democrats (TBB) and the conservatives (TGB). The former focuses on secularism, women's rights and recognition of Turkish community as a minority, while the latter appeals to those who favour wearing headscarves in public places, teaching Islam in public schools and maintaining Turkishness. TBB began as part of a student movement at the Technical University of Berlin, campaigning for equal rights for international students, especially Turkish students. TBB is a top-down intellectual interest organisation, whereas TGB is a grass roots organisation, established by local Turkish businessmen. The leaders of TBB mostly came from the left-wing student organisation *Berlin Türk Bilim ve Teknoloji Merkezi* (BTBTM), which was Berlin's most influential Turkish left-wing organisation in the 1980s (Yurdakul, 2006, 440-448).

TBB established strong relationships with several leftist Turkish groups, whereas the leaders of TGB came from *Diyanet* organisations. TBB emphasizes that its policies and campaigns are directed towards Germany. It does not make public statements about Turkey or Turkish politics. TGB was established by local activists in Kreuzberg, including local entrepreneurs. It supports the idea of transnational politics, believing that the Turkish community remains tied to its homeland and affected by socio-political changes in Turkey. While the website of TBB is just in German, the one of TGB is mostly in German but some parts of it are also translated in Turkish. Many German political authorities refer to TBB and TGB as supporters of 'immigrant integration'. While TGB emphasizes Turkishness and Sunni Islam as the main unifying factor binding Turkish community together, TBB argues that Turks should become German citizens. TBB and TGB have rarely cooperated, except on a couple of campaigns, such as a press release in favour of dual citizenship on 12 January 1999. TGB organized 'Turkish March' on 27 May 2003. For this event, Turkish community from different German *lander* came together in Berlin (Yurdakul, 2006: 440-448). However, it has not been sustained because of conflicts between different Turkish community organisations.

Most of the interviewees emphasized that they do not prefer to be referred to as Turkish immigrants, but rather as German-Turks. Because many of them were born in Germany and some of them are German citizens. As Sinan Kaplan (2012), the chairman of UETD-Berlin[2] (Union of European Turkish Democrats) argued, there are 6,000 entrepreneurs in Germany. It is wrong to refer to them as immigrants, as a third of them were born here. While the first generation was immigrants, most of them had already died.

Kenan Kolat (2012), the head of the Turkish Community in Germany (Türkische Gemeinde Deutschlands - TGD), which was established in 1995, emphasized that TGD is not a diaspora organisation: 'We emerged firstly to defend the rights and interests of Turkish community; gradually we have also started to defend the rights of other immigrants. We are gradually becoming a human rights organisation too. If we will only become a human rights organisation we would break our ties with Turkish community'. Therefore, they prefer to remain positioned between being a Turkish community organisation and a human rights organisation. Kolat

[2] UETD was established in 2004. Its goal is political cooperation between Germany and Turkey. It has 52 branches. They encourage the new generations who graduated from university in Germany to participate in German politics.

(2012) noted that TGD is an umbrella organisation that includes approximately 300 sub-units, claiming that it is the most influential institution of Turkish community in Germany. He acknowledged that other Turkish community organisations can also be successful but argued that their main agenda is usually related with Turkey, or focuses on cultural and ethnic characteristics of the community. TGD's agenda is tried to be set by ourselves'. As he puts it:

When German state wants to deal with the problems here they usually contact with TGD and the associations that are members of TGD. We are overrepresented in German public opinion compared to the strength of our basis. The main problem is to what extent you can mobilize them for rights and to solve the problems of Turkish community. TGD has three main goals. The first is for citizens to live together in German society with equal rights. The second is to fight against racism, Islamophobia, Turcophobia and anti-semitism. The third is to support Turkey's EU membership bid from the perspective of Turkish community in Germany. TGD is in favour of Turkey's EU membership, emphasizing the practical benefits of membership on the daily lives of Turkish community in Germany, such as their right to vote locally, if they were not German citizens. It also emphasizes importance of the membership for building bridges between Christian and Muslim communities (Böttger and Maggi, 2009: 39-44).

Until 2003, there were no immigrant advisory councils in Berlin, and few opportunities for Turkish community organisations to influence policy-making. In particular, Islamic organisations had few opportunities to communicate with local authorities in Berlin. However, individual linkages were formed between Turkish organisations and local politicians. For example, TBB has personal links with the SPD. The political influence of Turkish community organisations has remained relatively low, although umbrella organisations such as TBB and TGB are more visible than others and have more contacts with local politicians. In 2006, Berlin made its approach toward immigrant groups more accommodative. Since then, immigrant organisation advisory councils have been established, an official integration policy framework has been introduced and senator has been appointed for integration affairs. These measures have increased the political incorporation of Turkish community organisations into Berlin's political system (Vermeulen and Berger, 2011: 181-187).

The main focuses of Turkish community organisations in Berlin are integration, dual citizenship, and fighting discrimination and racism. Ahmet İyidirli (2012), the former head of another umbrella organisation Social Democrat Public Associations, is currently working as the head of *Tiyatrom* (*Türkisches Theater Berlin*) argues that when we look at the main focuses of Turkish community organisations over the last thirty years, the proportion of issues related to Turkey has been decreasing. Because the new generations have been socialised in Germany, they usually do not follow or understand Turkish politics. Turkish community organisations' main focuses have therefore moved to Germany, including gaining equal rights, to be recognized as German in terms of social status, and solving problems about education and working life. According to İyidirli (2012), Turkish community organisations can help, host and immigrant societies to come together culturally and socially through youth exchanges. Ercan Karakoyun (2012), the head of Forum of Intercultural Dialogue (FİD) in Berlin, suggested that the most problematic place regarding integration and adaptation issues is Berlin.

The level of cooperation among Turkish community organisations in Berlin is very low. According to İyidirli (2012), the emergence of these organizations started mostly in the second half of the 1970s, when political tensions were particularly high in Turkey. There was almost no dialogue between these competing parties. As a result of their experiences in Germany and increasing self-confidence of the organisations, there has been increasing dialogue among them. İyidirli (2012) claimed that in order to establish better dialogue between these organisations, professionalisation is needed, arguing that currently 'we exchange our views when we come together but there are no established structures which encourage this cooperation'. Meanwhile, German state's approach is usually religiously focused, as they mostly prefer to communicate with Turkish community organisations to discuss problems of immigrants as Muslims.

The issue of dual citizenship is one of the main problems for Turkish community, according most of the interviewees. Kolat, and other like-minded leaders of Turkish community organisations, wished for Turkish community to receive German citizenship to create a mass of potential voters. This would allow them to put pressure on Germany's political parties to force them to pay attention to the problems of German citizens, with Turkish backgrounds (Yurdakul, 2006: 447). Kaplan (2012) notes that participation in German elections is very low among Turkish community, adding that when Turkish community organisations invite people to meetings, attendance is also very low. Consequently, it is impossible to collect 50,000 signatures needed to ask for a change in the citizenship law. Yılmaz (2012) suggests that the problem of dual citizenship could be solved by a change in Turkish law, so that Turkish citizens would not lose Turkish citizenship if they took another country's citizenship.

Turkish community organisations in Berlin usually maintain close relations with German political parties, especially the Christian Democrats and the Social Democrats. However, they rarely cooperate with German CSOs and Turkish CSOs in Turkey. Kaplan (2012) points out that:

We support in political terms the organisations which have integration and adaptation courses. In our board of directors we have those, who work in *Bundestag*. We are in contact with all German political parties except the extreme ones.

Kaplan (2012) argues that, rather than German CSOs, they have closer relations with German political parties and rarely cooperate with Turkish CSOs. Muzaffer Türk (2012), the General Secretary of MÜSİAD (Independent Industrialists and Businessmen Association) Berlin[3], stated that they cooperate closely with other branches of MÜSİAD in Europe, with MÜSİAD Turkey being their closest partner. MÜSİAD Berlin aims to promote the entrepreneurial activities of its members and negotiations between smaller Turkish businesses and German economic and political institutions. It also deals with integration of Turkish community and political integration of Turkey into EU (Amelina and Faist, 2008: 106-107). Yılmaz (2012) argued that they have close relations with German political parties, even closer than Turkish political parties, in particular with

[3] It was established in 1994 by second generation Turkish businessmen in Germany after the establishment of MÜSİAD in Turkey in 1990. It does not have any organic ties with MÜSİAD in Turkey but they have close relations.

CDU and SPD. He mentioned that Turkish community organisations have low levels of communication and cooperation with Turkish CSOs, while few of the interviewees mentioned communicating or cooperating with German civil society either, although Karakoyun (2012) stated that they communicate with German CSOs. He added that ideological polarisation is still going on among Turkish community organisations, to an even greater extent than in Turkey. Karakoyun put forward that, Turkish community organisations also fear communicating with German civil society in case they become assimilated. Kolat (2012) stated that on the contrary, their organisation has close relations with German CSOs, including the unions, business organisations, churches and Jewish Central Council. He added that they cooperate also at a European level, including Turkish organisations and umbrella organisations. He claimed that they apply for all types of funds, including those provided by local authorities and the EU. He put forward that there is a 'zero-sum-game' mentality among Turkish community organisations. On the contrary to this mentality, he mentioned a change in his organisation's regulations. According to that, 'four out of nine members of our executive council can be chosen from outside. They can participate in our meetings without having a right to vote. If it is successful, they may become members in the future'. He commented that they usually cooperate with foundations in Turkey, such as TESEV, the Social Democracy Foundation, and that they are planning to improve their cooperation with Turkish CSOs in the future. However, he claimed that cooperation with Turkish community organisations is not on the agenda of Turkish CSOs in Turkey, although many things can be done together.

One of the main problems for Turkish community organisations in Berlin is professionalisation. İyidirli (2012) argues that most of the leaders of these organisations, except the religious organisations, are not professional, so their directors have a lot of work to do. As Yılmaz (2012) mentioned, the level of cooperation among Turkish community organisations in Berlin is low because they see each other as competitors, so in order to guarantee themselves in financial terms, they compete with each other to get funds. However, if they could cooperate with each other, they could get funds for bigger projects. He reported that 'we are also giving education to these organisations to become professional. Many of them have deficiencies in terms of personnel and they do not have experience about how to do projects'.

Jan Taşçı (2012) from Network Turkey[4], an academic network of academics from Turkey and Germany, whose studies focus on Turkey, stated that there is a growing interest about Turkey in Germany among both academicians and the public. He argued that it is easier to come together in an academic atmosphere. Taşçı (2012) noted that when Turkey is discussed in Germany, the main focus is Turkish community in Germany, rather than Turkey itself.

Şen (2012) claimed that, because of the rise of Islamophobia and Turcophobia in Germany, Turkish community organisations have become more introverted. For example, when there was a debate about a ban on circumcision, Turkish Islamic Union for Religious Affairs (DİTİB) could not say anything, whereas the Jewish community criticized the proposal harshly. Kolat (2012) argued that Turkish community organisations in Germany cannot act together to fight extreme-right violence against Turkish community. Yılmaz (2012) also criticized the fact that Turkish community organisations could not organise large demonstrations. He added that religious organisations are usually more able to come together. Thus, one of the biggest challenges for Turkish community organisations is that they rarely act together for common goals, which decreases their influence in German politics.

Thus, there are several deficiencies of Turkish community organisations including their low level of professionalisation, cooperation among each other, high level of polarisation among them which have negatively affected their influence in German politics.

The Role of Turkish Community Organisations in Berlin in Turkey-EU Relations and Their Perceptions about Turkey's EU Membership Bid

Turkish community organisations are not so influential in Germany, because of their deficiencies mentioned above, thus, they

[4] Network Turkey was a student initiative which started at the Free University of Berlin before moving to Humboldt University. They organise workshops for those who study Turkish studies both in Germany and throughout Europe.

do not have a strong influence in Turkey-Germany and Turkey-EU relations. Turkish community organisations mostly support Turkey's EU membership bid, primarily because it will positively affect Turkish immigrants without German citizenship. In 2002, the *Europaisch-Türkischen Zivil platform* (ETZ) was founded by various Turkish community organisations in Europe, with TGD as the leading organization and TBB playing a central role. TGB is also a member of this platform. Its main goal is to gain political recognition for Turkish immigrants at European level and lobbying for Turkey's accession to EU. For example, its local members collected signatures from Turkish immigrants living in various European cities to support Turkey's EU membership bid (Yurdakul, 2006: 448).

Turkish-German Business Association Berlin-Brandenburg (*Türk-Alman Birliği Berlin-Brandenburg* - TDU) deals with both economic and political issues, seeing itself as the link between German political and economic institutions and Turkish community. It liaises with other Turkish community organisations such as TGD, particularly regarding integration of Turkish immigrants, and granting dual citizenship. TDU also supports Turkey's EU accession. For example, in June 2004, before the European Parliament (EP) elections, it appealed to its members to vote only for parties that support EU membership for Turkey (Amelina and Faist, 2008: 109).

Şen (2012) argues that Turkish community organisations are mostly very positive about Turkey's EU membership. According to his research in 2008, 78% of Turkish community supports this, because they would like to have equality with the Greek and Spanish communities in Germany, who benefit from several rights, such as free movement of people and participating in elections if they are living in another EU country. However, he believes that Turkish community organisations currently have little influence in Germany. Kaplan (2012) argues that almost all Turkish community organisations are in favour of Turkey's EU membership, except one or two. He added that neither the idea of a 'privileged partnership' nor Turkey's EU membership is the focus of German politics.

İyidirli (2012) commented that in recent years, the EU has been off the political agenda in both Turkey and Germany, as both sides have been focusing on their own internal problems. Before elections in Germany, the Social Democrats and the Greens both try to highlight the point that, if Turkey can fulfil several conditions, they are in favour of Turkey's membership, in order to gain votes from Turkish community.

Türk (2012) stated that Turkish community feels as if they are in EU, particularly the businessmen. His organisation has expressed its concerns to German politicians about visa facilitation for Turkish businessmen and its importance for economic relations between Turkey and Germany. If Turkey becomes an EU member, Turkish businessmen in Germany will cooperate more with Turkish businessmen in Turkey which will also contribute to German economy.

Türk (2012) claimed that 'we can influence German politicians more at the local level, but far less at the federal level'. Karakoyun (2012) argued that during non-election periods nobody wants to talk about the question of Turkey's EU membership. However, during election campaigns, anti-Turkey, anti-Islam discourse increased in Germany. He predicted that EU membership for Turkey could also have positive psychological effects on Turkish community. Regarding the role of Turkish community organisations in Turkey and Germany and Turkey-EU relations, Yılmaz (2012) argued that, although Turkish community is large, it does not have much influence in Germany, although its economic strength has increased. As he put it, 'we are high in number but we have a low number of people in terms of quality. There are few people in high positions...the voters from Turks are few'. He stated that if Turkey becomes an EU member, the members of Turkish community can gain the right to vote after staying in any member state for six months. He commented that this will increase Turkey's influence within EU.

While the EU has provided Germany's Greek, Italian and Spanish communities with the instruments to incorporate themselves into the German polity, it has not for German-Turks (Ögelman *et al.*, 2002: 156). According to Kolat (2012), Turkey's EU membership will provide new rights for Turkish community, such as free movement of people, participation in local and European Parliament (EP) elections, dual citizenship and work in public institutions. He emphasized that they look at the process from the perspective of Turkish community, stating that the main two items on their agenda is fighting racism and electoral participation. 'We proposed for the first time the concept of 'participation' rather than 'integration'. He also argued that 'we have to participate even when we are not similar, but of course we have to adapt', adding that obstacles related to education, culture, religion and vocational education for participation of Turkish community need to be abolished.

For İyidirli (2012), it is difficult for Turkish community organisations to get EU funds because there is a highly competitive atmosphere. He stated that 'German CSOs do not need Turkish community organisations for the EU projects. They usually ask us if we can recommend any Turkish CSO in Turkey'. Because, they need a partner CSO from another EU country or a candidate country like Turkey. Turkish community organisations sometimes apply to European Social Fund. The heads of Turkish community organisations usually work voluntarily rather than professionally, making it hard for them to compete in the project market. İyidirli (2012) suggested that, if Germany does not help to professionalise Turkish community organisations then Turkey should. Turkey could allocate funds for certain types of projects for these organisations. He added that 'the structure of these organisations has to be strengthened. If they have a strong structure, they can get more financial resources'.

As a result, Turkish community organisations in Berlin usually see each other as competitors, rarely cooperate with Turkish CSOs in Turkey and German CSOs. They have closer communication with German political parties, especially the CDU and SPD. They are mostly in favour of Turkey's EU membership especially because of the benefits that will be gained by the Turkish community in Germany who does not have a German citizenship. However, their influence in German politics is low, thus, they do not have a strong influence in German foreign policy towards Turkey's EU membership bid.

Conclusion

The Turkish community in Germany is not monolithic but highly fragmented and polarised, which means groups are often unable to work together effectively to reach common goals, such as for greater political empowerment or dual citizenship (Ögelman *et al.*, 2002: 152). As Ögelman *et al.* (2002: 146-156) argue, German politicians usually seem to be ignorant about the foreign policy preferences of Turkish immigrants, who are not mobilized as an effective lobby to make their voices heard in Germany. The German polity and the Turkish divisiveness constrain the political influence of German-Turks. The main item on German foreign policy agenda regarding Turkey is its EU membership process. Turkish community has a limited access to German politics, and it is fragmented, so its influence on German foreign policy has been almost nothing.

There is a gap between Turkish community organisations in Berlin and German civil society organisations. They also rarely cooperate with Turkish civil society organisations in Turkey, while Turkish community organisations usually do not cooperate with each other too. Instead, they usually see each other as competitors, having closer communication with German political parties, especially the CDU and SPD.

Turkish community organisations in Berlin could play a crucial role both in integrating Turkish immigrants contributing to solving socio-cultural and economic problems of Turkish community. They mostly support Turkey's EU membership bid, not only because Turkey is their country of origin, rather because of interests of the Turkish community in Germany. Turkish community organisations in Berlin are mostly unprofessional and highly polarised ideologically, which makes it hard for them to act together for common goals, or as a bridge between Turkey and Germany, or between Turkey and the EU. In order to be more influential in German politics, they have to be professionalized and they have to cooperate more with German and Turkish CSOs. Turkey should provide funding for projects between Turkish community organisations and Turkish CSOs that contribute to socio-economic improvement of Turkish community. On the other hand, Germany should encourage cooperation and provide more funding for projects between Turkish community organisations and German CSOs, which would contribute to solving the integration problems Turkish community. Meanwhile, Turkish community organisations have to cooperate more with each other by overcoming their ideological rivalries in order to find solutions for the common problems of Turkish Community in Germany, which would also increase their influence in German politics and they could contribute more to Turkey-Germany and Turkey-EU relations.

Acknowledgements:

The interviews were conducted by the author with the scholarship provided by the Free University of Berlin Department of Political and Social Sciences KFG (Transformative Power of Europe) in September 2012.

Interviews conducted by the author:

Interview with Bakır, S. (September 5, 2012) Chairman of Turkish German Chamber of Commerce and Industry (TD-İHK), Berlin.

Interview with İyidirli, A. (18 September 2012) The head of Tiyatrom(TürkischesTheater Berlin), Berlin.

Interview with Kaplan, S. (7 September 2012) The chairman of UETD-Berlin (Union of European Turkish Democrats), Berlin.

Interview with Karakoyun, E. (19 September 2012) The head of Forum of Intercultural Dialogue (FİD) in Berlin, Berlin.

Interview with Kolat, K. (12 September 2012) The head of Turkish Community in Germany (TürkischeGemeindeDeutschlands-TGD), Berlin.

Interview with Strachwitz, R. (6 September 2012) Director of MaecenataInstitute of Humboldt University, Berlin.

Interview with Şen, F. (24 July 2012) The head of the board of directors of TAVAK (Turk-German Education and Scientific Research) Foundation, İstanbul.

Interview with Taşçı, J. (20 September 2012) Network Turkey, Berlin.

Interview with Türk, M. (20 September 2012) the General Secretary of MÜSİAD Berlin, Berlin.

Interview with Yılmaz, H. (11 September 2012) The head of the Union of Craftsmen and Artisans of Berlin (TUH) and Akarsu Association, Berlin.

References

Abadan-Unat, N. (1997). Ethnic Business, Ethnic Communities, and Ethno-politics Among Turks in Europe in E. M. Ucarer & D. J. Puchala (Eds). *Immigration into Western Societies*. London: Pinter.

Abella, M., & Ducanes, G. (2009). The effect of the global economic crisis on Asian migrant workers and government responses. *Asian and Pacific Migration Journal*, 18(1), 143.

Alba, R. (2005). Bright vs. blurred boundaries: Second-generation assimilation and exclusion in France, Germany, and the United States, *Ethnic and Racial Studies*, 28(1), 20-49.

Ambrosini, M. (2013). *Irregular Migration and invisible*, Welfare, Palgrave Macmillan.

Amelina, A. & Faist, T. (2008). 'Turkish migrant associations in Germany: between integration pressure and transnational linkages', *Pratiques Transnationales-Mobiliteet Territorialites*, 24 (2): 91-120.

Amir-Moazami, S. (2007). *Politisierte Religion. Der Kopftuchstreit in Deutschland und Frankreich*. Bielefeld: transcript Verlag.

Amnesty International. (2009). Stranded: Refugees in Turkey Denied Protection. Retrieved 11.02.2011, from http://www.unhcr.org/refworld/docid/49f018842.html

Anderson, B. (1992). Long-Distance Nationalism: World Capitalism and the Rise of Identity Politics. Amsterdam: Centre for Asian Studies Amsterdam.

Apap, J. (2002). Shaping Europe's Migration Policy New Regimes for the Employment of Third Country Nationals: A Comparison of Strategies Germany, Sweden, the Netherlands and the UK. *European Journal of Migration and Law*, 4, 309-328.

Appadurai, A. (2006). *Fear of Small Numbers: An Essay on the Geography of Anger*. Durham: Duke University Press.

Atalay, P. (2014, October 6). Interview by E.J. Rothchild. Hamburg, Germany.

Atikon, E. (2006). Citizenship or Denizenship: the Treatment of Thrid Country Nationals in the European Union, SEI Working Paper, No. 85, Sussex European Institute, http://www.sussex.ac.uk/sei/. Available on: 09.06.2014.

Avci, G. (2005). Religion, Transnationalism and Turks in Europe. *Turkish Studies*, 6 (2), 201-213.

Bade, K. (2013). *Kritik und Gewalt: Sarrazin-Debatte, ‚Islamkritik' und Terror in der Einwanderungsgesellschaft* [Criticism and Violence: Sarrazin Debate, Criticism of Islam and Terror in the Immigration Society]. Schwalbach: Wochenschau Verlag (in German).

Baklacioglu, N. O. (2009). Building 'Fortress Turkey' Europeanization of Asylum Policy in Turkey. *The Romanian Journal of European Studies, 7-8* (Special Issue: South-Eastern Europe and the European Migration System: East West Mobility in Flux), 103-118.

Balibar, E. (1998). Propositions on Citizenship. *Ethnics*, 98(4), 723-730.

Basch, L., Glick-Schiller, N., and Blanc, C. S. (1994). *Nations Unbound: Transnational Projects, Postcolonial Predicaments, and Deterritorialized Nation-States*. London and New York: Routledge.

Bayraktaroğlu-Özçelik, G. (2013). Yabancılar ve Uluslararası Koruma Kanunu Hükümleri Uyarınca Yabancıların Türkiye'den Sınır Dışı Edilmesi, *Türkiye Barolar Birliği Dergisi*, 103, 211-258.

Benhabib, S. (2004). *The Rights of Others: Aliens, Residents and Citizens*. United Kingdom, Cambridge: University Press

Benhabib, S. (2006). *Ötekilerin Haklari: Yabancilar, Yerliler, Vatandaşlar. (The Rights of Others: Foreigners, Nationals, Citizens.)* B. Akkiyal (Translator). İstanbul: İletişim Yayınları. (In Turkish, Original Work Published in 2004).

Berechet, B., & Tuncay, B. (2013). Trafficking for Labour Exploitation-Origin, Transit and Destination Countries. *Pub. Sec. Stud.*, 2, 123.

Bernard, T. (2003). Türk Müslümanlar ve Devlet Aşırı Alanın Toplumsal Kanalları Olarak İslami Örgütler. (Turkish Muslims and Islamic Organizations as the Social Channels of Trans-National Spaces). In: T. Faist (Eds.), S. Dingiloğlu (Translator) *Devletaşırı Alan: Almanya ve Türkiye Arasında Siyaset, Ticaret ve Kültür (Trans-national Space: Politics, Trade and Culture between Germany and Turkey)*. İstanbul: Bağlam, pp.57-80.

Biehl, K. (2009). Migration 'Securitization'and its Everyday Implications: An Examination of Turkish Asylum Policy and Practice. Paper presented at the Euro-Mediterranean Consortium for Applied Research on International Migration (CARIM).

Bilgiç E. E. & Kafkaslı, Z. (2013). Gencim, Özgürlükçüyüm, Ne İstiyorum? [I am Young, I am Libertarian, What do I Want?]. Received from http://www.bilgiyay.com/Content/files/DIRENGEZI.pdf available on: 27.07.2014.

Bloch, A. (2012). *Irregular Migrants: Policy, Politics, Motives and Everyday Lives*. London: Routledge

Bloch, A. & Chimenti, M. (2011). Irregular Migration in a globalizing word, *Ethnic and Racial Studies*, 34 (8), 1271-1285.

Bloemraad, I. (2013). Accessing the Corridors of Power: Puzzles and Pathways to Understanding Minority Representation. *West European Politics*, 36(3), 652-670.

Bloemraad, I., & Schönwälder, K. (2013). Immigrant and Ethnic Minority Representation in Europe: Conceptual Challenges and Theoretical Approaches. *West European Politics*, 36(3), 564-579.

Boswell, C. (2003). *European Migration Policies in Flux: Changing Patterns of Inclusion and Exclusion*. Oxford: Blackwell Publishing Ltd.

Böttger, K. and Maggi, E.M. (2009). 'German perceptions'. In: SaitAkşitet al. (eds.) *Turkey Watch: EU Member States' Perceptions on Turkey's Accession to the EU, Strengthening and Integrating Academic Networks (SınAN)*, Ankara: Centre for European Studies, Middle East Technical University: 32-45.

Brandt, A., Meyer, C., Neubacher, A., Neumann, C., Schießl, M., Schmidt, C., and Ulrich, A. (2004, November 15). Für uns gelten keine Gesetze [For Us No Laws Apply]. *Der Spiegel*, p. 60 (in German).

Brinkbäumer, K., Cziesche, D., Mascolo, G., Meyer C., & Ulrich, A. (2001, November 26). Die Krieger aus Pearl Harburg [The Warriors from Pearl Harburg]. *Der Spiegel*, p. 40-70 (in German).

Brubaker, R. (1992). *Citizenship and Nationhood in France and Germany*. Cambridge, Mass: Harvard University Press.

Bulaç, A. (1998). Avrupa'nin "Öteki" ile Bir Arada Yaşama Tecrübesi. (The Experience of Europe with the 'Other') Zor Diyalog: Türkiye ve Almanya (Tough Dialogue: Turkey and Germany) İstanbul: Ege Yayinları. (In Turkish).

Çaglar-Şimsek, A. (2002). A Table in Two Hands. D. Kandiyoti & A. Saktanber (Eds.), Fragments of Culture, New Jersey: Rutgers University Press.

Calavita, K. (2010). *Inside the State: The Bracero Program, Immigration, and the INS*. Quid Pro Books.

Carens, J. (2008). The rights of Irregular Migrants, *Ethics and International Affairs*, 22 (2), 163-186.

Castel, S. & Miller M. J. (2010). *The age of Migration. International Population Movements in the modern World*. London, Palgrave.

Castells, M. (2008). The New Public Sphere: Global Civil Society, Communication Networks, and Global Governance. *The ANNALS of the American Academy of Political and Social Science*, 616, 78-93.

Castles, S. and Miller, M.J. (2010). Migration and Global Economic Crisis: One Year On, Virtual Symposium, Retrieved from http://www.age-of-migration.com/ uk/financialcrisis/updates/migration_crisis_april2010.pdf, on 3, March, 2014.

Castles, S. & Davidson, A. (2000). *Citizenship and Migration: Globalization and the Politics of Belonging*. London: Macmillan.

Castles, S. & Miller, M. J. (1998). *The Age of Migration: International Population Movements in the Modern World*. New York: Guildford Press.

Catterall, B. (2013). Towards the Great Transformation: (7) Locating Gezi Park. *City*, 17 (3), 419-422.

Cellamare, G. (2012). *Lezioni sulla disciplina irregolare*, Torino: Giappichelli Editore.

Cevik, H. H., & Demirci, S. (2008). *Kamu Politikasi, Kavramlar, Aktorler, Surec, Modeller, Analiz, Karar Verme*. Ankara: Seckin.

Cholewinsky, R. (2007). *The legal Status of Migrants admitted for Employment Committee of experts on Legal Status and Rights of Immigrants; a comparative Study of Law and Practice in selected European States*. Council of Europe: Publishing.

Çiçekli, B. (2009). *Uluslararası Hukukta Mülteciler ve Sığınmacılar*. Ankara.

Claude, R. P. & Weston, B. H. (2006). *Human Rights in the World Community*, University of Pennsylvania Press.

Crawford, M. (2008). Gender and the Australian parliament. PhD thesis, Queensland University of Technology. Online available at:

http://eprints.qut.edu.au/26409/1/Mary_Crawford_Thesis.pdf# (last access: 25.05.2014)

Cziesche, D., Hipp, D., Kurz, F., Schmid, B., Schreiber, M., Sümening, M., Tyburski, S., and Ulrich, A. (2003, September 29). Das Kreuz mit dem Koran [The Cross with the Koran]. *Der Spiegel*, p. 82-97 (in German).

Dardağan-Kibar, E. (2012). "Yabancılar ve Uluslararası Koruma Kanunu Tasarısında ve Başlıca Avrupa Birliği Düzenlemelerinde Yabancıların Sınır Dışı Edilmesine İlişkin Kurallar: Bir Karşılaştırma Denemesi" *Ankara Avrupa Araştırmaları Dergisi*, 11 (2), 53-74.

Davies, R. (2000). Neither Here nor There? The Implications of Global Diasporas for (inter)national Security. D. T. Graham & N.K. Poku (Eds), *Migration, Globalisation and Human Security*. London: Routledge.

Dell'olio, F. (2005). *The Europeanization of Citizenship between the Ideology of Nationality, Immigration, and European Identity*. Bulington: Ashgate.

Dembour, M. & Kelly, T. (2011). *Are Human Rights for Migrants? Critical Reflections on the status of irregular migrants in Europe and United States*. Abigdon, Routledge

Diehl, C. & Blohm, M. (2003). Rights or Identity? Naturalization Process among 'Labor Migrants' in Germany. *International Migration Review*, 37 (1), 133-162.

Diehl, C. & Blohm, M. (2011). Naturalization as boundary crossing: Evidence from labour migrants in Germany. In: Assaad Elia Azzi, Xenia Chryssochoou, Bert Klandermans and Bernd Simon (Eds), *Identity and participation in culturally diverse societies: a multidisciplinary perspective*. Oxford: Wiley-Blackwell.

Donnelly, J. (1999). The Social Construction of International Human Rights. In (Ed.) T. Dunne & N.J. Wheeler, *Human Rights in Global Politics*. Cambridge: Cambridge University Press.

Dorr, S. and Faist, T. (1997). Institutional Condition for the Integration of Immigrants in Welfare States: A Comparison of the Literature on Germany, France, Great Britain and the Netherlands. *European Journal of Political Research*, 31, 421-426.

Dover, R. (2008). "Towards a Common EU immigration policy: a securitization too far", in *European Integration,* 3 0(1), 113-130.

Durgun, S. (2002). Turk Kamu Yonetiminde Burokratik Siyaset *G.U.I.I.B.F, Special Issue* 83-102.

Durgun, S. & Yayman, H. (2005). The Turkish Bureaucracy as a Guardian of Statist Tradition. In R. S. Salmi & G. B. Durgun (Eds.), *Turkish-US Relations:Perspectives from Ankara,* Florida.

Ekşi, N. (2008). "İnsan Hakları Avrupa Mahkemesi Kararlarında Sığınmacı ve Mültecilerin Türkiye'den Sınır Dışı Edilmelerini Engelleyen Haller", *İstanbul Barosu Dergisi*, 82 (6) 2803-2837.

El-Enay, N. (2013). EU Asylum, Immigration and Border Control Regimes: including and excluding the Deserving Migrant, *European Journal Social Security*, 171.

Engelen, E. (2006). Towards an Explanation of the Performance Differences of Turks in the Netherlands and Germany: The Case of a Comparative Political Economy of Integration. *Royal Dutch Geographical Society*, 97 (1), 69-79.

Ergüven, S. N. & Özturhanlı, B. (2013). "Uluslararası Mülteci Hukuku ve Türkiye", *Ankara Üniversitesi Hukuk Fakültesi Dergisi*, 62 (4), 1007-1061.

Eryilmaz, B. (2010). *Bürokrasi ve Siyaset: Bürokratik Devletten Etkin Yönetime* (4 ed.): Alfa Basım Yayım Dağıtım Limited Sti.

Estrada-Tank, D. (2013). Human Security and the Human Rights of Undocumented migrants: systematic vulnerabilities and obligations of protection, *European Journal of Social Security*, 15 (2), 151-170.

European Union, European Commission, Progress Report (2012). Turkey 2012 Progress Report accompanying with the document of Communication from the Commission to the European Parliament and the Council, Enlargement Strategy and Main Challenges 2012-2013. Retrieved from http://ec.europa.eu/enlargement/ countries/detailed-country-information/turkey/index_en.htm.

Faist, T. (1994). Immigration, Integration and the Ethnicization of Politics: A Review of German Literature. *European Journal of Political Research*, 25, 439-459.

Faist, T. (2000). *The Volume and Dynamics of International Migration and Transnational Social Spaces*. Oxford: Oxford University Press.

Faist, T. (2003). *Uluslararası Göç ve Ulusaşırı Toplumsal Alanlar. (International Migration and Trans-national Social Spaces)* A.Z. Gündoğan & C. Nacar (Translators.) Istanbul: Baglam Yayincilik. (Original Work Published in 2000 by Oxford University Press.) (In Turkish).

Faist, T. (2013). "Multiculturalism: From heterogeneities to social (in) equalities" in *Debating Multiculturalism in the Nordic Welfare States*, p. 22.

Farmer, A. (2008). "Non-Refoulement and Jus Cogens: Limiting Anti-Terror Measures that Threaten Refugee Protection", *Georgetown Immigration Law Journal*, 23(1), pp.1-38.

Fekete, L. (2009). *A Suitable Enemy: Racism, Migration and Islamophobia in Europe*. London/New York: Pluto Press.

Fisek, K. (1982). The Bonapartist Origins and Failings of Central Provincial State Administration in Turkey - A Case Study in Administrative Transplantation In UNESCO (Ed.), *Public Administration and Management: Problems of Adaptation in Different Socio-Cultural Contexts*. UNESCO, pp. 110-125.

Fix, M., Papademetriou, D.G., Terrazas, A., Yi-Ying Lin S. & Mittelstadt M. (2009). *Migration and the Global Recession*. Washington, DC: Migration Policy Institute and BBC World Service.

Flikschuh, K. (2010). Kant's Sovereignty Dilemma: A Contemporary Analysis, *The Journal of Political Philosophy*, 18 (4), p.469-493.

Follath, E. (2001, June 2). Die Macht des Propheten [The Power of the Prophet]. *Der Spiegel*, p. 158-178 (in German).

Fouron, G. E. & Glick-Schiller, N. (2002). The Generation of Identity: Redefining the Second Generation within a Transnational Social Field. In Levitt P. &

Waters M. C. (eds.) *The Changing Face of Home: The Transnational Lives of the Second Generation.* New York: Russel Sage Foundation. pp. 168-210.
Frelick, B. (1997). Barriers to Protection: Turkey's Asylum Regulations. *International Journal of Refugee Law*, 9 (1).
Fukuyama, F. (2002). Social Capital and Development: The Coming Agenda. *The SAIS Review of International Affairs*, 22(1), 23-37.
Gallup (2011, December 7).) African, Gulf States Most Positive About Muslim-West Relations. *Gallup World.* Received from http://www.gallup.com/poll/151352 /african-gulf-states-positive-muslim-west-relations.aspx available on: 07.12.2011.
Garfinkel H. (1967). *Studies in Ethnomethodology*. New Jersey: Prentice-Hall.
Geddes, A. (2000). *Immigration and European Integration: Towards a Fortress Europe?* New York: Manchester University Press.
Geddes, A. (2003). *The Politics of Migration and Immigration in Europe*: Sage Publications Limited.
Genç, N. (2013). Rise of Turkish Citizens' Media. *Index on Censorship*, 42, 92-95.
Gerdes, J. (2003). Çifte Pasaport, Devletaşırılık, Çokkültürcülük ve Çifte Yurttaslik. In: T. Faist (Ed.), *Devletasirı Alan: Almanya ve Turkiye Arasinda Siyaset, Ticaret ve Kültür*. S. Dingiloğlu (Translator). İstanbul: Bağlam Yayıncılık.
Gewirth, A. (1996). The Community of Rights. In Minkler L. (2013), *The State of Economic and Social Human Rights: A Global Overview*. The USA: Cambridge University Press.
Giraud, M. (2000). Cultural Identity and Migrations. In R. Hudson & F. Reno (Eds.), *Politics of Identity: Migrants and Minorities in Multicultural States.* Hampshire: Palgrave.
Gitmez, A. S. (1983). *Yurtdışına İşçi Göçü ve Geri Dönüşler*. Istanbul: Alan Yayınları.
Glaser, B. & Strauss, A. L. (1967) *The Discovery of Grounded Theory: Strategies for Qualitative Research.* Chicago: Aldine Publishing Company.
Glick-Schiller, N., Basch, L. and Blanc-Szanton, C. (1992). Transnationalism: A New Analytic Framework for Understanding Migration. *Annuals of the New York Academy of Sciences*, 645, pp.1-24.
Goffman, E. (1959). *The presentation of self in everyday life*. Garden City, N.Y: Doubleday.
Goffman, E. (1963). *Stigma: Notes on the Management of Spoiled Identity.* Englewood Cliffs, NJ: Prentice Hall.
Göktürk, D., Gramling, D., and Kaes, A. (2007). *Germany In Transit: Nation and Migration 1955-2005*. Berkeley: University of California Press.
Göle, N. (2013). Gezi – Anatomy of a Public Square Movement. *Insight Turkey*, 15 (3), 7-14.
Graglia, D. (2009). Immigration and the Global Recession: Debate Heating up in Australia & the UK. In Tilly, C. (2011), *The Impact of the Economic Crisis on International Migration: Review, in Work, Employment and Society*. 25(4): 675-692.

Gräner, M. (2013, 7 November). SPD macht Druck bei doppelter Staatsbürgerschaft [SPD puts pressure on double citizenship]. *Sozialdemokratische Partei Deutschlands (SPD)*. Received from http://www.spd.de/aktuelles/111528/20131107_ag_inneres_ und_recht.html available on: 26.11.2013 (in German).

Graziano T. (2012). The Tunisian Diaspora: Between "Digital Riots" and Web Activism, *Social Science Information*, 51 (4), 534-550.

Green, T. & Winters, L.A. (2010). Economic Crisis and Migration: Learning From the Past and the Present. Working Paper T31, *Development Research Centre on Migration*. Brighton: University of Sussex.

Greene, R.A. & Torre, I. (2014, September 1). "Syria's foreign jihadis: Where do they come from?" *CNN.com*. Received from http://edition.cnn.com/interactive/ 2014/09/syria-foreign-jihadis/_available on: 01.09.2014.

Greschke H. M. (2012). Is There a Home in Cyberspace?: The Internet in Migrants' Everyday Life and the Emergence of Global Communities. New York: Routledge.

Güleç, C. (2013, June 25). Interview by E. J. Rothchild. Digital Recording. Hamburg, Germany.

Hailbronner, K. (2000). *Immigration and asylum how and policy of the European Union*, The Hague, Kluwer law International.

Hailbronner. K. (Ed.) (2010). *European Immigration and Asylum Law*. UK: Hart Publishing. www.hartpub.co.uk/books/details.asp?isbn=9781849460750

Halfmann, J. (1997). Immigration and Citizenship in Germany: Contemporary Dilemmas. Political Studies, XLV, 260-274.

Hammarbeg, T. (2009). It is wrong to criminalize Migration, *European journal of Migration and Law*, 11, 383-385.

Hartnell, H.E. (2006). Belonging: Citizenship and Migration in the European Union and in Germany. *Berkeley Journal of International Law*, 24 (1), 330-400.

Harvey D. (2012). *Rebel Cities: From the Right to the City to the Urban Revolution.* London and New York: Verso.

Healther, J. (2013). Multifaceted Migration Management: bilateral Mobility Partnership in the European Union. *George Washington International Law Review*, 45(2), 383-414.

Held, D. (2002). The Law of States, Law of Peoples; Three Models of Sovereignty. *Legal Theory*. 8 (2), p. 43-97.

Held, D. (2010). Principles of Cosmopolitan Order. In: Garett, W. & Held, D. *The Cosmopolitanism Reader*. Cambridge: Polity Press

Heper, M. (1976). Political Modernization as Reflected in Bureaucratic Change: The Turkish Bureaucracy and a" Historical Bureaucratic Empire" Tradition. *Int. J. Middle East Stud*, 7(4), 507-521.

Heper, M. (2010). *Türkiye'de Devlet Gelenegi (The State Tradition in Turkey).* Ankara.

Hoeppner, A. (2013, September 30). Interview by E.J. Rothchild. Digital Recording. Hamburg, Germany

Humphrey, M. (2009). 'Securitisation and domestication of diaspora Muslims and Islam: Turkish immigrants in Germany and Australia', *International Journal on Multicultural Societies*, 11 (2), 136-154.

ILO (1975). *C143-Migrant Workers (Supplementary Provisions) Convention*. Retrieved from http://www.ilo.org/dyn/normlex/en/f?p=NORMLEXPUB:55:0:::55:P55_TYPE,P55_LANG,P55_DOCUMENT,P55_NODE:SUP,en,C143,/Document

ILO (2009). *Strengthening Migration Governance-Implementation of OECD Commitments related to migration by OECD participating States.* Retrieved from http://www.ilo.org/migrant/publications/WCMS_204168/lang--en/index.htm. Jointly published by ILO and OSCE.

ILO (2012). *ILO Constitution Preamble.* Retrieved from http://www.ilo.org/dyn/normlex/en/f?p=1000:62:0::NO:62:P62_LIST_ENTRIE_ID:2453907:NO#A4 on 2 November 2013.

ILO (International Labour Organisation) (1949). *CO97-Migration for Employment Convention (Revised), 1949 (No.97)*. Retrieved from http://www.ilo.org/dyn/normlex/en/f?p=NORMLEXPUB:12100:0::NO:12100:P12100_ILO_CODE:C097 on 4 November 2013.

Itzigsohn J., Cabral D. C., Medina E. H. and Vazquez O. (1999). Mapping Dominican Transnationalism: Narrow and Broad Transnational Practices. *Ethnic and Racial Studies*, 22 (2), 316-339.

Jacobson, D. (1996). *Rights across Borders: Immigration and the Decline of Citizenship*. Baltimore: Johns Hopkins University Press.

Kabaalioglu, H. & Eksi, N. (2004). "Yabancıların Türkiye'den Sınırdışı Edilmesi", *Milletlerarası Hukuk ve Milletlerarası Özel Hukuk Bülteni*, 24(1-2), 503-522.

Kadioglu, A. (1992). Citizenship, Immigration and Racism in a Unified Germany with Special Reference to the Turkish Guestworkers. *Journal of Economics and Administrative Studies*, 6 (1-2), 199-211.

Kadioglu, A. (1997). Is Racism Being Combated Effectively in Germany? The New Immigration Legislation. In: G. Rystad (Eds.), *Encountering Strangers: Responses and Consequences*. Lund: Lund University Press. pp. 73-92.

Kaiser, K. (1971). Transnational Politics: Toward a Theory of Multinational Politics. *International Organization*, 25 (4), 790-817.

Kale, B. (2005). The Impact of Europeanisation on Domestic Policy Structures: Asylum and Refugee Policies in Turkey's Accession Process to the European Union. PhD, Middle East Technical University: Ankara.

Kant, I. [1795] (1923). Zum Ewige Frieden: Ein philosophischer Entwurf. In Benhabib, S. (2004). *The Rights of Others: Aliens, Residents and Citizens*. United Kingdom: Cambridge University Press.

Kant, I. [1795] (1970a). Perpetual Peace: A Philosophical Sketch. Trans. By H. B. Nisbett. In: *Kant: Political Writings*. Ed. by Hans Reiss. UK: Cambridge University Press.

Kant, I. [1797] (1978). *Moral Law: Kant's Groundwork of the Metaphysics of Morals*. Trans. Paton, H.J. London: Hutchinson & Co Publishers.

Karagöz, H. (2009). *Küresel Ekonomik Kriz ve Alınan Ekonomik Tedbirler*. Konya: Trade Chambers Publication.

Kastoryano, R. (2002). *Negotiating identities: States and immigrants in France and Germany*. Princeton University Press.

Kaya, A. and Kentel, F. (2005). *Euro-Türkler: Türkiye ve Avrupa Birliği Arasında Köprü mü, Engel mi? (Euro-Turks: A Breech or a Bridge between Turkey or the European Union?).* Istanbul: Bilgi Universitesi Yayınları. (In Turkish).

Kaya, A. (2000). *'Sicher in Kreuzberg' Berlin 'deki Kucuk Istanbul: Diasporada Kimliğin Oluşumu. (Sicher in Kreuzberg, Little Istanbul in Berlin: the Formation of Identity in Diaspora)* Istanbul: Buke Ltd. Sti. (In Turkish).

Kaya, A. (2001). *Sicher in Kreuzberg: Constructing Diasporas: Turkish Hip-Hop Youth in Berlin*. Bielefeld: transcript Verlag.

Kaya, A. & Kentel, F. (2005). *Euro-Turks: A Bridge or a Breach between Turkey and the EU? A Comparative Study of German-Turks and French-Turks*, Brussels: Centre for European Policy Studies.

Kaya, I. (2009). *Reform in Turkish Asylum Law: Adopting the EU acquis?* , European University Institute Robert Schuman Centre for Advance Studies.

Kaya, I. (2012). Seeking a Legal Perspective on International Migration and Turkey. *International Refugee Law, 8*(3), 293-318.

Kelle, U. (2006). Computer-assisted qualitative data analysis. In: Clive Seale, Giampetro Gobo, Jaber F. Gubrium and David Silverman (Eds), *Qualitative Research Practive*. London: Sage.

Kelle, U. & Kluge, S. (2010). *Vom Einzelfall zum Typus. Fallvergleich und Fallkontrastierung in der qualitativen Sozialforschung (2nd Ed.).* Opladen: Leske+Budrich.

Kessler, A.E. & Freeman, G. P. (2005). Public Opinion in the EU on Immigration from Outside the Community. *Journal of Common Market Studies*, 43(4), 825-850.

Kirisci, K. (1996). Coerced Immigrants: Refugees of Turkish Origins since 1945, *International Migration*. 34(3), 385-412.

Kirisci, K. (2001). UNHCR and Turkey: Cooperating for Improved Implementation of the 1951 Convention Relating to the Status of Refugees. *International Journal of Refugee* Law, 13, 71-97.

Kirisci, K. (2002). Immigration and Asylum Issues in EU–Turkish Relations: Assessing EU's Impact on Turkish Policy and Practice'. In S. Lavenex & E. M. Uçarer (Eds.), *Migration and the Externalities of European Integration* (pp. 125-142).

Kirisci, K. (2003). The Question of Asylum and Illegal Migration in European Union-Turkish Relations. *Turkish Studies,* 4(1), 79-106.

Kirisci, K. (2004a). *Asylum, Immigration, Irregular Migration and Internally Displacement in Turkey: Institutions and Policies* Paper presented at the Euro-Mediterranean Consortium for Applied Research on International Migration (CARIM). Analytic and Synthetic Notes - Political and Social Module European University Institute, Robert Schuman Centre for Advanced Studies.

Kirisci, K. (2004b). Reconciling Refugee Protection with Combating Irregular Migration: Turkey and the EU Perceptions. *Journal of International Affairs,* 9, 1-13.

Kirisci, K. (2005). A Friendlier Schengen Visa System as a Tool of Soft Power: The Experience of Turkey. *European Journal of Migration and Law*, 7(4), 343–367.

Kirisci, K. (2007). Turkey: A Country of Transition from Emigration to Immigration. *Mediterranean politics,* 12(1), 91-97.

Kirisci, K. (2012). Turkey's New Draft Law on Asylum: What to Make of It? In S. P. Elitok & T. Straubhaar (Eds.), *Turkey, Migration and the EU: Potentials, Challenges and Opportunities* (pp. 63-85). Hamburg: Hamburg University Press.

Kivisto, P. & Faist, T. (2010). *Beyond a border: the causes and consequences of contemporary immigration.* Oaks, Pine Forge Press.

Kluge, S. (2000). Empirically Grounded Construction of Types and Typologies in Qualitative Social Research, *Forum Qualitative Social Research*, 1(1).

Kösemen, O. (2013). Wenn aus Ausländern Wähler werden: Die ambivalente Rolle der Parteien beider Repräsentation von Migranten in Deutschland. http://mediendienstintegration.de.

Koser, K. (2010). Dimensions and dynamics of irregular migration, *Population, Space and Place*, 16 (3), 181-193.

Kosnick K. (2000). Building Bridges: Media for Migrants and the Public-Service Mission in Germany. *European Journal of Cultural Studies*, 3 (3): 319-342.

Kosnick K. (2007a). Ethnic Media, Transnational Politics: Turkish Migrant Media in Germany. Bailey O. G., Georgiou M., Harindranath R. (eds.) *Transnational Lives and the Media: Re-Imagining Diaspora.* Hampshire and New York: Palgrave Macmillan, 149-172.

Kosnick K. (2007b). *Migrant Media: Turkish Broadcasting and Multicultural Politics in Berlin.* Bloomington: Indiana University Press.

Kurthen, H. (1997). Defining the Fatherland: Immigration and Nationhood in Pre- and Postunification Germany. R. Alter & P. Monteath (Eds.), *Rewriting the German Past: History and Identity in the New Germany*. New Jersey: Humanities Press International. pp. 65-102.

Kuyumlu M. B. (2013). Reclaiming the Right to the City: Reflections on the Urban Uprisings in Turkey. *City*, 17 (3), 274-278.

Kwong. P. (1999). *Forbidden Workers. Illegal Chinese Immigrants and American Labor*. New Press.

Kymlicka, W. & Norman, W. (2000). Citizenship in Culturally Diverse Societies: Issues, Contexts, Concepts. W. Kymlicka & W. Norman (Eds.), *Citizenship in Diverse Societies*. New York: Oxford University Press.

Kymlicka, W. & Norman, W. (1994). Return of the Citizen: A Survey of Recent Work on Citizenship Theory. *Ethics*, 104, 352-381.

Lamont, M. & Virág, M. (2002). The Study of Boundaries in the Social Sciences, *Annual Review of Sociology*, 28, 167-195.

Landolt, P. (2008). The Transnational Geographies of Immigrant Politics: Insights from a Comparative Study of Migrants Grassroots Organizing. *The Sociological Quarterly*, 49, 53-77.

Latham, R. & Sassen, S. (2005). Introduction: Digital Formations: Constructing an Object of Study. Latham R. and Sassen S. (eds.) *Digital Formations: IT and New Architectures in the Global Realm*. New Jersey: Princeton University Press. pp. 1-34.

Lauterpacht, S. E. & Bethlehem, D. (2003). "The Scope and Content of the Principle of Non-refoulement". In: *Refugee Protection in International Law: UNHCR Global Consultations on International Protection*, eds. Feller, E., Türk, V. & Nicholson, F., Cambridge, pp. 87-177.

Law, J. & Martin, E.A. (2009). *(7th Edition) Oxford Dictionary of Law*, New York, Oxford University Press

Lefebvre, H. (1991). *The Production of Space*, Oxford and Cambridge MA: Blackwell.

Lefebvre, H. (1996). *Writing on Cities*. Oxford and Malden: Blackwell.

Lemert. C. C. (2005). *Social Things: An Introduction to the Sociological Life*. Rowman & Littlefield.

Levitt, P. & Jaworsky, B. N. (2007). Transnational Migration Studies: Past Developments and Future Trends. *Annual Review of Sociology*, 33, 129-156.

Levitt, P. & Schiller, N. G. (2004). Conceptualizing Simultaneity: A Transnational Social Field Perspective on Society. *International Migration Review*, 38 (3), 1002-1039.

Lovenduski, J. & Norris, P. (1993). *Gender and party politics*. Sage Publications Limited.

Lovenduski, J. & Norris, P. (1996). *Women in Politics.* Oxford University Press

Mahler S. (1998). Theoretical and Empirical Contributions toward a Research Agenda for Transnationalism. In: Smith M. P. and Guarnizo L. E. (eds.) *Transnationalism From Below, Comparative Urban & Community Research.* New Brunswick and New Jersey: Transaction Publishers. pp. 64-102.

Mandel, R. (2008). *Cosmopolitan Anxieties. Turkish Challenges to Citizenship and Belonging in Germany*. Durham: Duke University Press.

Mann, I. (2013). Dialectic of Transnationalism: Unauthorized Migration and Human Rights, *Harvard International Law Journal*, 54 (2), 315-392.

Mansbridge, J. (2004). Representation Revisited: Introduction to the Case Against Electoral Accountability. *Democracy and Society*, 2(1), 12-13.

Mansbridge, J. (1999). Should blacks represent blacks and women represent women? A contingent yes. *Journal of Politics*, 61(3), 628-657.

Marcus, G. E. (1995). Ethnography in/of the World System: The Emergence of Multi-Sited Ethnography. *Annual Review of Anthropology*, 24, 95-117.

Marshall, T. H. (1950). Citizenship and Social Class, In:. Goodin & P. Pettit (Eds), *Contemporary Political Philosophy: An Anthology*. Oxford: Blackwell Publishers Ltd, pp. 291-319.

Martin, P. (2004a) Germany: Managing Migration in the 21st Century. In: Cornelius, Wayne A., Takeyuki Tsuda, Philip L. Martin, and James F.

Hollifield. (Eds.) *Controlling Immigration. A Global Perspective*. CA: Stanford University Press, pp. 221-252.

Martin, P. (2004b). The United States: The Continuing Immigration Debate. In: Cornelius, Wayne A., Takeyuki Tsuda, Philip L. Martin, and James F. Hollifield. (Eds.) *Controlling Immigration. A Global Perspective*. CA: Stanford University Press, pp. 51-85.

Martin, P. (2009), Recession and Migration: A New Era for Labour Migration? *International Migration Review*, 43 (3), 671-691.

Martin, S. (2010). *A Nation of Immigrants*. MA: Cambridge University Press.

Mäs, M., Mühler, K., and Opp, K. (2005). When are individuals called "German"? Empirical results of a factorial survey, *Kölner Zeitschrift Für Soziologie und Sozialpsychologie*, 57(1), 112-134.

McCabe, K. & Meissner, D. (2010). *Immigration the United States: Recession affects flows, prospects for reform*. Washington DC, Migration Information Source. Retrieved from http://www.migrationinformation.org/Profiles/display.cfm?ID=766.

McNamara, F. (2013). Member State responsibility for Migration Control within Third States – Externalization Revisited, *European Journal of Migration and Law*, 15(3), 319-338.

Michon, L. & Vermeulen, F. (2013). Explaining Different Trajectories in Immigrant Political Integration: Moroccans and Turks in Amsterdam. *West European Politics*, 36(3), 597-614.

Migrant Integration. (2011, May). Qualitative Eurobarometer Aggregate Report for the European Commission.

Migration News (1999). Welfare Down, California Poll. 6(2), February. http://migration.ucdavis.edu/mn/more.php?id=1720_0_2_0.

Migration News. (1996). Welfare Overhaul and Minimum Wage Changes. 3(9), September. http://migration.ucdavis.edu/mn/more.php?id=1022_0_2_0.

Miller, D. (2008). Irregular Migrants: an Alternative Perspective, *Ethics and International Affairs*, Vol. 22, 2, p. 193-197.

Miller-Idriss, Cynthia (2006). Everyday Understandings of Citizenship in Germany, *Citizenship Studies*, 10(5), 541-570.

Ministry of Interior Asylum and Migration Bureau. (n.d.). Tasks of the Bureau Retrieved 20.03.2013, from http://gib.icisleri.gov.tr/default_B0.aspx?content=1002.

Minkler L. (2013). *The State of Economic and Social Human Rights: A Global Overview*. MA: Cambridge University Press.

Mitra A. & Watts E. (2002). Theorizing Cyberspace: The Idea of Voice Applied to the Internet Discourse. *New Media & Society*, 4 (4), 479-498.

Modood, T., Triandafyllidou, A., & Zapata-Barrero, R. (2006). European challenges to multicultural citizenship. In: Modood, T., Triandafyllidou, A., & Zapata-Barrero, R. (eds.) *Multiculturalism, Muslims and Citizenship: A European Approach*. London and New York: Routledge. pp. 1-22.

Morris, L. (2000). Rights and Controls in the Management of Migration: The Case of Germany. *Sociological Review*, 225-240.

Morticelli, A. and Guth, J. (2012). 'European Union Law Approaches to Illegal Immigration – An Overview of Legislative Provisions'. Illegal Immigration: Comparing National Legal Frameworks in Italy and the UK – Phase 1A report. Bradford University Law School [online] available at http://www.brad.ac.uk/management/research/groups/law/.

Moscheen in Hamburg [Mosques in Hamburg]. (2013). *moscheesuche.de.* Received from http://www.moscheesuche.de/moschee/stadt/Hamburg/1488 available on: 22.03.2014.

Mügge L. (2010). *Beyond Dutch Borders: Transnational Politics among Colonial Migrants, Guest Workers and the Second Generation.* Amsterdam: Amsterdam University Press.

Munz, R. (2003). Migration and demographic change in Europe. In: Von Offman, Bernd (eds.) Towards a Common European Immigration Policy. Reports and Discussions of a Symposium held in Trier on October 24th and 25th, 2002, Frankfurt am Main, S. 11.

Münz, R., Ulrich, R. (1997). Changing Patterns of Immigration to Germany, 1945-1995: Ethnic Origins, Demographic Structure, Future Prospects. In: KJ. Bade & M. Weiner (Eds.), *Migration Past, Migration Future: Germany and the United States*. Berghahn Books.

Nisbet E. C., Stoycheff E. & Pearce K. E. (2012). Internet Use and Democratic Demands: A Multinational, Multilevel Model of Internet Use and Citizen Attitudes about Democracy. *Journal of Communication*, 62 (2), 249-265.

Norris, P. & Lovenduski, J. (1995). *Political recruitment.* Cambridge University Press.

Nuhoğlu-Soysal, Y. (1994). *Limits of Citizenship: Migrants and Postnational Membership in Europe*. Chicago: University of Chicago Press.

Odmalm, P. (2009). 'Turkish organizations in Europe: how national contexts provide different avenues for participation', *Turkish Studies*, 10 (2): 149-163.

OECD (Organisation for Economic Co-Operation and Development) (2009). *International Migration Outlook 2009,* OECD elibrary. Retrieved from http://www.oecd-ilibrary.org/social-issues-migration-health/international-migration-outlook-2009/international-migration-and-the-economic-crisis_migr_outlook-2009-3-en, accessed on 22-03-2014.

Ögelman N. (2005). Immigrant Organizations and the Globalization of Turkey's Domestic Politics, Koslowsky R. (ed.) *International Migration and the Globalization of Domestic Politics.* New York and London: Routledge. pp. 33-61.

Ogelman, N. (2003). 'Documenting and explaining the persistence of homeland politics among Germany's Turks', *International Migration Review*, 37 (1): 163-193.

Ögelman, N., et al. (Summer-Fall 2002). 'Immigrant cohesion and political access in influencing foreign policy', *SAIS Review*, 22 (2): 145-165.

Örs İ. R. (2014). Genie in the Bottle: Gezi Park, Taksim Squere, and the Realignment of Democracy and Space in Turkey. *Philosophy & Social Criticism*, (published online before print) March 6 2014, DOI: 10.1177/0191453714525390.

Østergaard-Nielsen E. (2003a). The Politics of Migrants' Transnational Political Practices. *International Migration Review*, 37 (3), 760-786.

Østergaard-Nielsen E. (2003b). *Transnational Politics: Turks and Kurds in Germany*. London and New York: Routledge.

Ostergaard-Nielsen, E. (2000). 'Trans-state loyalties and politics of Turks and Kurds in Western Europe', *SAIS Review*, 20 (1): 23-38.

Ozbudun, E. (2000). *Contemporary Turkish Politics: Challenges to Democratic Consolidation*. London: Lynne Rienner Pub.

Özyer, B. (2013). Gezi Park Protests around the Clock #historyrecordedlive. Received from: http://yasarkenyazilantarih.com/historyrecordedlive/#p=20 on: 25.07.2014.

Papademetriou, D. G., Sumption, M., & Somerville, W. (2009). *Migration and the economic downturn: what to expect in the European Union*. Migration Policy Institute.

Paulus, S. (2007). Einblicke in fremde Welten. Orientalische Selbst/ Fremdkonstruktionen in TV-Dokumentationen über Muslime in Deutschland [Insights into Foreign Worlds. Oriental Self/Foreign constructions in TV documentaries about Muslims in Germany]. Attia, I. (ed.) *Orient und IslamBilder: Interdisziplinäre Beiträge zu Orientalismus und antimuslimischen Rassismus* [Orient and Images of Islam: Interdisciplinary Contributions to Orientalism and Anti-Muslim Racism]. Münster: Unrast. pp. 279-292 (in German).

Pence, A. (2013, November 26). Interview by E.J. Rothchild. Digital Recording. Hamburg, Germany.

Peter, F. (2010). Welcoming Muslims into the nation: Tolerance, politics and integration in Germany. In: Cesari, J. (ed.) *Muslims in the West after 9/11: Religion, Politics and Law*. London and New York: Routledge. pp. 119-144.

Philipps, A. (1994). "Dealing With Difference: A Politics of Ideas or A Politics of Presence?" *Constellations*, 1(1), pp. 88-91.

Philipps, A. (1995). *The Politics of Presence*. Oxford: Oxford University Press.

Pirjola, J. (2007). Shadows in Paradise- Exploring Non-Refoulement as an Open Concept. *International Journal of Refugee Law*, 19 (4), 639-660.

Pitkin, H. F. (1967). *The Concept of Representation*. Berkeley: University of California Press.

Pop, A. (2008). European Union Initiatives in tackling Migration and Organized Crime At its New Eastern Borders, *Romanian Journal of 4 European Affairs*, 8(1), 45-59.

Powell Jr, G. B. (2004) Political representation in comparative politics, *Annual Review of Political Science*, 7, 273-296.

Pries, L. (1999). New Migration in Transnational Space. Pries L. (ed.) *Migration and Transnational Social Spaces.* Aldershot: Ashgate.
Prümm, K. (2004). *Einbürgerung als Option: die Bedeutung des Wechsels der Staatsangehörigkeit für Menschen türkischer Herkunft in Deutschland.* Münster:LIT.
Pustu, Y. (2007). Osmanli-Turk Geleneginde Modernlestirici Unsur Olarak Burokratik Elitler (Bureaucratic Elites as Agents of Modernization in the Ottooman-Turkish State Regime). *Gazi University Journal of Economics and Administrative Sciences, 9*(2), 197-214.
Putnam, R. D. (2000). *Bowling Alone: The Collapse and Revival of American Community.* New York: Simon & Schuster Paperbacks.
Rawls, J. (1999). *The Law of Peoples.* Cambridge, Mass.: Harvard University Press.
Regionalergebnisse – Stand 29.06.2011. (2011). *Der Norden zählt.* Received from http://www.statistik-nord.de/fileadmin/regional/regional.php available on: 24.10.2013.
Religionsgemeinschaften: Hamburg unterzeichnet Staatsvertrag mit Muslimen und Aleviten [Religious Communities: Hamburg Signs State Treaty with Muslims and Alevis]. (2012, November 13). *Spiegel Online.* Received from http://www.spiegel.de/politik/deutschland/hamburg-unterzeichnet-staatsvertrag-mit-muslimen-und-aleviten-a-867032.html available on: 29.10.2013 (in German).
Robins, K. & Webster, F. (1999). *Times of the Techno Culture: From the Information Society to the Virtual Life.* London and New York: Routledge.
Robins, P. (2009). Public Policy Making in Turkey: Faltering Attempts to Generate a National Drugs Policy. *Policy & Politics,* 37(2), 289-306.
Rosello, M. (2001). *Postcolonial hospitality: the immigrant as guest.* Stanford University Press.
Rosenau J. N. (1969). Toward the Study of National-International Linkages. In: Rosenau J. N. (ed.) *Linkage Politics: Essays on the Convergence of National and International Systems.* New York: Free Press. pp. 44-63.
Rosenbach, M. & Stark, H. (2011, May 7). Eine Bombe für Deutschland [A Bomb for Germany]. *Der Spiegel,* p. 28-33 (in German).
Rosenhek, Z. (2000). Migration Regimes, Intra-State Conflicts, and the Politics of Exclusion and Inclusion: Migrant Workers in the Israeli Welfare State. Journal of *Soial. Problems, 47,* 49-67.
Ross, C. (2013). *The EU and Immigration policies: cracks in the wall of fortress Europe?* London: Palgrave.
Rotte, R. (2000). Immigration Control in United Germany: Toward a Broader Scope of National Policies. *International Migration Review,* 34 (2), 357-389.
Ruhs, M., and Martin, P. (2008). Numbers vs. Rights: Trade-offs and Guest Worker Programs. *International Migration Review.* 42(1), pp.249-65.
Ruhs, M. (2013). *The Price of Rights: Regulating International Labour Migration.* Princeton: Princeton University Press.
Sacks, H. (1995). *Lectures on Conversation Volume I & II.* Oxford: Blackwell.

Sahin-Mencutek, Z. (2012). Immigration Control in Transit States: The Case of Turkey. *European Journal of Economic and Political Studies,* 5, 1.

Sassen S. (1996). *Losing Control? Sovereignty in an Age of Globalization.* New York: Columbia University Press.

Sassen, S. (2003). Globalization or Denationalization? *Review of International Political Economy*, 10 (1), 1-22.

Sassen, S. (2006). *Territory, Authority, Rights: From Medieval to Global Assemblages.* Princeton and Oxford: Princeton University Press.

Sassen, S. (1999). *Guests and Aliens*. New York: New Press.

Sawyer, C. (2011). *Statelessness in the European Union: displaced, undocumented, unwanted.* Cambridge University Press.

Schiffer, S. (2008). Islam in German Media. Al-Harmarneh, A. & Thielmann, J. (eds.) *Islam and Muslims in Germany*. Leiden and Boston: Brill. pp. 423-440.

Schneider, B. R. (1992). *Politics within the State: Elite Bureaucrats and Industrial Policy in Authoritarian.* Brazil: University of Pittsburgh Press.

Schneider, J. (2002). Discourses of Exclusion: Dominant Self-Definitions and "The Other" In German Society, *Journal of the Society for the Anthropology of Europe*, 2(1), 13-21.

Schoeneberg, U. (Autumn 1985) 'Participation in ethnic associations: the case of immigrants in West Germany', *International Migration Review*, 19 (3): 416-437.

Schrep, B. (2014, September 22). Nur Himmel oder Hölle [Only Heaven or Hell]. *Der Spiegel*, p. 38-41 (in German).

Şeker, G. & Özer, B. (2014). Kamu Yönetiminde İstenmeyen Yabancıları Sınır Dışı Etme Faaliyeti ve Kolluk Uygulaması. In: D. Danış, & İ. Soysüren (eds), *Sınır ve Sınırdışı. Yabancıların Sınır Dışı Edilmesi ve Sınır Üzerine Disiplinlerarası Bakışlar*. İstanbul: Nota Bene Yayınları, pp. 402-426.

Selm, J. V. (2005). Where Migration Policy is Made. Starting to Expose the Labyrinth of National Institutional Settings for Migration Policy Making and Implementation. *Global Migration Perspectives*, 37. Switzerland: Global Commission on International Migration.

Sezgin, Z. (2011). 'Turkish migrants' organizations in Germany and their role in the flow of remittances to Turkey', *International Migration and Integration*, 12, 231-251.

Shooman, Y. & Spielhaus, R. (2007). The concept of the Muslim enemy in the public discourse. Cesari, J. (ed.) *Muslims in the West after 9/11: Religion, Politics, and Law*. London and New York: Routledge. pp. 198-228.

Silverman D. (2001). *Interpreting Qualitative Data: Methods for Analysing Talk, Text and Interaction.* London and Thousand Oaks and New Delhi: Sage.

Sirkeci, I. (2003). *Migration, Ethnicity and Conflict.* Doctoral dissertation, University of Sheffield.

Sirkeci, I. (2006). *The environment of insecurity in Turkey and the emigration of Turkish Kurds to Germany.* New York and Lampeter: Edwin Mellen Press.

Sirkeci, I. (2009). Transnational mobility and conflict. *Migration Letters*, 6(1), 3-14.

Sirkeci, I. & Cohen, J.H. (2015). Cultures of migration and conflict in contemporary human mobility in Turkey. *European Review*, 22(2) (forthcoming).
Sirkeci, I., & Martin, P. L. (2014). Sources of Irregularity and Managing Migration: The Case of Turkey. *Border Crossing: Transnational Working Papers*, No.1401, 1-16.
Smith, M. P. (1994). Can You Imagine? Transnational Migration and the Globalization of Grassroots Politics. *Social Text*, 39, 15-33.
Soysal Y. N. (1994). *Limits of Citizenship: Migrants and Postnational Membership in Europe.* Chicago: The University of Chicago Press.
Spiegel Online (2010, October 17). Integrationsdebatte: "Multikulti ist eine erfolgreiche Realität" [Integration Debate: "Multiculturalism is a Successful Reality"]. *Spiegel Online*. Received from http://www.spiegel.de/politik/deutschland/ 0,1518,723589,00.html available on: 28.11.2010 (in German).
Spiegel Online. (2011). Spiegel Online: Das Nachrichtenportal im Internet. Report for *Spiegel Online*, p. 1-12.
Spielhaus, R. (2006). Religion and identity. How Germany's foreigners have become Muslims. *Internationale Politik Transatlantic Edition*, 8(2), 17-23.
Staples, H. (1999). *The legal Status of Third Country Nationals Resident in the European Union* (Vol. 22). The Hague: Kluwer law international.
Statistisches Bundesamt. (2013a). Fachserie 1 Reihe 2.1. Ausländische Bevölkerung. Ergebnisse des Ausländerzentralregisters. Wiesbaden.
Statistisches Bundesamt. (2013b). Fachserie 1 Reihe 2.1. Bevölkerung und Erwerbstätigkeit. Einbürgerungen 2012. Wiesbaden.
Stoyanova, V. (2008-2009). The Principle of Non-Refoulement and the Right of Asylum-Seekers to Enter State Territory", *Interdisciplinary Journal of Human Rights Law*, 3 (1), 1-11.
Supp, B. (2006, July 3). Die Integrierten [The Integrated]. *Der Spiegel,* p. 58-63 (in German).
Swain, C. M. (1993). *Black Faces, Black Interests: The Representation of African Americans in Congress.* Cambridge, MA: Harvard University Press.
Taneri, G. (2012). *Uluslararası Hukukta Mülteci ve Sığınmacıların Geri Gönderilmemesi*. Ankara.
Taras, R. (2012). The End to Immigration by a Thousand Cut? On Europe's Bureaucratic Gatekeepers (Vol. 1): Malmö University, Malmö Institute for Studies of Migration, Diversity and Welfare (MIM) Willy Brandt Series of Working Papers in International Migration and Ethnic Relations.
Tetik, N. (2012). Global Economic Crisis: Experience of Turkey as the Model of Recovery. *Journal of Academic Research in Economics*. 4 (1), 36-50.
Thym, D. (2004). Reforming Europe's common foreign and security policy, *European Law Journal*, 10(1), 5-22.
Thym, D. (2013). EU migration policy and its constitutional national: a cosmopolitan outlook, *Common Market Law Review*, 50(3), 709-736.
Tilly, C. (2011). The Impact of the Economic Crisis on International Migration: Review. *Work, Employment and Society*, 25(4), 675-692.

Togeby, L. (2004). It Depends… How Organizational Participation Affects Political Participation and Social Trust among Second-Generation Immigrants in Denmark, *Journal of Ethnic and Migration Studies*, 30 (3), 509-528.

Tolay, J. (2012). Coming and Going: Migration and Changes in Turkish Foreign Policy. In: R. L. et.al. (Ed.), *Turkey and Its Neighbors Foreign Relations in Transition* (pp. 119-143). UK: Lynne Rienner.

Torpey, J. (1999). *The Invention of the Passport: Surveillance, Citizenship and the State*. MA: Cambridge University Press.

Triandafyllidou, A. (2010). *Irregular migration in Europe: Myths and Realities*, Farnham Surrey: Ashgate, UK.

Triandafyllidou, A., Maraoukis, T., (2012). *Migrant smuggling: irregular migration from Asia and Africa to Europe*, Palgrave: Macmillan.

Turner, B. S. (2001). The Erosion of Citizenship. *British Journal of Sociology*, 52(2), 189-209.

UN. (1991). International Convention on the Protection of the Rights of All Migrant Workers and Members of Their Families (ICRMW) (1991). Special Issue: UN. *International Migration Review*. 25 (4):873-919

Uzun, E. (2012). "Geri Göndermeme (Non – Refoulement) İlkesinin Uluslararası Hukuktaki Konumu Üzerine bir Değerlendirme", *Uluslararası Hukuk ve Politika*, 8(30), pp. 25-58.

Vasta, E. (2011). Immigrants and the paper market: borrowing, renting and buying identities, *Ethnic and Racial Studies*, 34(2), 187-206.

Verba, S., Schlozman, K. L., and Brady, H. E. (1995). *Voice and equality: Civic voluntarism in American politics*. (Vol. 4). Cambridge, MA: Harvard University Press.

Vermeulen, F. (2013). 'Mutualism, Resource Competition, and Opposing Movements among Turkish Organizations in Amsterdam and Berlin', 1965-2000, *British Journal of Sociology*, 64(3), 453-477.

Vermeulen, F. (2008). *Diversiteit in Uitvoering. Lokaal beleid voor werkloze migrantenjongeren in Amsterdam en Berlijn*. Den Haag: NICIS Institute.

Vermeulen, F. & Berger, M. (2011). 'Civic networks and political behavior: Turks in Amsterdam and Berlin'. In: S. Karthick Ramakrishnan and I. Bloemraad (eds), *Civic Hopes and Political Realities: Immigrants, Community Organisations and Political Engagement*. New York: Russell Sage Foundation: 160-192.

Waldinger, R. and Lichter, M. (2003). *How the Other Half Works: Immigration and the Social Organization of Labor*. CA: University of California Press.

Walker, M. (2010, October 12). Germans spar on immigration: Bavarian conservative leader suggests entry by Arabs, Turks should be limited. *The Wall Street Journal*, p. A14.

White, R., Donoghue, J. (2003). Marshall, Mannheim and Contested Citizenship. *British Journal of Sociology*, 54(3), 391-406.

Wiesbrok, A. (2010). *Legal Migration to the European Union*, Leiden: Nijhoff.

Winkler, M. (2011). "Il caso El Dridi al vaglio della Corte di Giustizia: verso una gestione più umana dei rimpatri di stranieri irregolari in Italia?" ("The El Dridi case pending before the Court of Justice: towards a more human repatriation of illegal foreigners in Italy?"). *Responsabilità civile e previdenza,* No. 7-8, p. 1485-1508.

Witte, N. (2014). Legal and symbolic membership. Symbolic boundaries and naturalization intentions of Turkish residents in Germany, *EUI/RSCAS Working Paper*, No. 100, 1-47.

Witzel, A. and Reiter, H. (2012). *The Problem-Centred Interview*. London: Sage.

Wolfsfeld G., Segev E., and Sheafer T. (2013). Social Media and the Arab Spring: Politics Comes First. *The International Journal of Press/Politics*, 18 (2), 115-137.

Worbs, S. (2003). The Second Generation in Germany: Between School and Labor Market. *International Migration Review*, 37(4), 1011-1038.

World Bank. (2012). Selected World Development Indicators 2012. *data.worldbank.org/sites/default/files/wdi-2012-ebook.pdf.*

World Bank. (2014). *Net Migration Data.* Retrieved from http://data.worldbank.org/indicator/SM.POP.NETM.

Wortham, S. & Rhodes, C. (2013). "Life as a chord: Heterogeneous resources in the social identification of one migrant girl." *Applied Linguistics*, 34(5), 536-553.

Wunderlich, T. (2005). *Die neuen Deutschen: subjektive Dimensionen des Einbürgerungsprozesses.* Stuttgart: Lucius & Lucius.

Wüst, A. M. (2011). "Migrants as parliamentary actors in Germany". In Karen Bird, Thomas Saalfeld and Andreas M. Wüst (eds.) *The Political Representation of Immigrants and Minorities. Voters, parties and parliaments in liberal democracies. Routledge.* NY. pp. 250-266.

Yalcindag, S. (1970). Kamu Yönetim Sistemimizin Tarihsel Evrimi Üzerine Notlar. *Amme Idaresi Dergisi* (2), 20-57.

Yurdakul, G. (2006). 'State, political parties and immigrant elites: Turkish immigrant associations in Berlin', *Journal of Ethnic and Migration Studies*, 32 (3), 435-453.

Yurdakul, G. (2009). *From Guest Workers into Muslims: The Transformation of Turkish Immigrant Associations in Germany*, Cambridge: Cambridge Scholars Pub.

Zieck, M. (2010). UNHCR and Turkey, and Beyond: of Parallel Tracks and Symptomatic Cracks. *International Journal of Refugee Law,* 22(4), 593-622.

Žižek S. (2013). Trouble in Paradise. *London Review of Books*, 35 (4), 11-12.

Zolberg, A. R. & Woon, L. L. (1999). Why Islam is like Spanish: Cultural Incorporation in Europe and the United States, *Politics & Society*, 27(1), 5-38.

Zuwanderer identifizieren sich mit Deutschland [Immigrants identify with Germany]. (2009, June 15). *Bertelsmann-Stiftung.* Received from http://www.bertelsmannstiftung.de/cps/rde/xchg/bst/hs.xsl/nachrichten_96355.htm available on: 01.05.2014.

CPSIA information can be obtained
at www.ICGtesting.com
Printed in the USA
LVHW090032130320
649951LV00001B/2/J

9 781910 781029